LITERACY, POLITICS, *and* ARTISTIC INNOVATION *in the* EARLY MEDIEVAL WEST

Papers Delivered at
"A Symposium on Early Medieval Culture"
Bryn Mawr College, Bryn Mawr, PA

Edited By Celia M. Chazelle

UNIVERSITY
PRESS OF
AMERICA

Lanham • New York • London

Copyright © 1992 by
University Press of America®, Inc.
4720 Boston Way
Lanham, Maryland 20706

3 Henrietta Street
London WC2E 8LU England

Library of Congress Cataloging-in-Publication Data

Symposium on Early Medieval Culture (1989 :
Bryn Mawr College)
Literacy, politics, and artistic innovation in the early
medieval west : a Symposium on Early Medieval Culture,
Bryn Mawr College, Bryn Mawr, PA /
edited by Celia M. Chazelle.
p.   cm.
1. Civilization, Medieval—Congresses.   2. Literacy—
Europe—History—Congresses.   3. Art, Medieval—
Congresses.   4. Literature, Medieval—History and
criticism—Congresses.   I. Title.
CB351.S95   1989   909.07—dc20   91–41660 CIP

ISBN 0–8191–8562–0 (cloth : alk. paper)
ISBN 0–8191–8563–9 (pbk. : alk. paper)

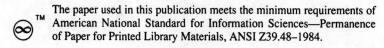

The paper used in this publication meets the minimum requirements of
American National Standard for Information Sciences—Permanence
of Paper for Printed Library Materials, ANSI Z39.48–1984.

Acknowledgments

Among the many people and institutions to whom I am grateful for their assistance in the production of this volume of essays, mention should be made first of The J. Paul Getty Trust which provided me with a post-doctoral fellowship at Bryn Mawr College in 1988-1989 and with funds to hold the symposium from which the volume has evolved. Bryn Mawr College must be thanked for so generously making facilities and equipment available for the meeting of the symposium in April 1989: for the lecture hall in which papers were delivered, for lending audio-visual equipment, and for the additional rooms where participants were able to gather informally between papers. Thanks are due, as well, to the members of The Delaware Valley Medieval Association and of the Bryn Mawr College community who turned out in such large numbers on a spring weekend to hear papers on what must have seemed, to some of them, a very obscure topic – early medieval culture. Special mention is necessary of the following individuals, for their particular assistance: the speakers themselves – Professors Seth Lerer of Stanford University, Thomas F.X. Noble of the University of Virginia, and Lawrence Nees of the University of Delaware – for their willingness to revise their papers for publication and for their help with production of the final manuscript; Professor Catherine Lafarge, Dean of the Graduate School of Bryn Mawr College, for her support and advice during the planning of the symposium and for delivering its opening remarks; Professor Dale Kinney of Bryn Mawr College for her patience and boundless good humor as I besieged her with virtually every problem encountered during preparation of the symposium; Professor Richard Hamilton, also of Bryn Mawr, for his sound advice on how to proceed with publication of the conference proceedings; Professor David Cast, at the time chair of the Art History Department at Bryn Mawr College; the department secretary, Mary Campo; and the department's graduate students. Finally, let me thank my husband Bernard, for his enormous assistance in preparing the final manuscript and for the countless other ways in which, as he well knows, he has aided me with this project.

Seth Lerer's article, reprinted here, first appeared in his book, *Literacy and Power in Anglo-Saxon Literature* (Lincoln, NE: University of Nebraska Press, 1991), and is reprinted by the kind permission of the University of Nebraska Press.

Table of Contents

Illustrations

Fig.1. Diagram by Charles Rufus Morey of the development of medieval style (after *Art Bulletin* 7 [1924]: 50)

Fig.2. Diagram by Alfred Barr of the development of modern art (after *Art Journal* 47 [1988]: 485)

Fig.3. Diagram by George Galavaris of the manuscripts of Gregory's Homilies (after Galavaris, *Gregory Nazianzenus*, 193 [full reference in Lawrence Nees, "Originality," n.16])

Fig.4. Comparison of illuminators in the Menologion of Basil II (after Weitzmann, *Roll and Codex*, pl. LV [full ref. in Nees, "Originality," n.15])

Fig.5. Wittislingen brooch, front (Munich, Prähistorische Sammlung) (courtesy of the Prähistorische Staatsammlung)

Fig.6. Wittislingen brooch, rear with inscription by Wigerig (courtesy of the Prähistorische Staatsammlung)

Fig.7. Godescalc Gospel Lectionary, colophon page (Paris, Bibliothèque Nationale, n.a. lat. 1203, fol. 126v) (courtesy of the Bibliothèque Nationale)

Fig.8. Godescalc Gospel Lectionary, Evangelist John and Christ (Paris, Bibliothèque Nationale, n.a. lat. 1203, fols. 2v-3r) (courtesy of the Bibliothèque Nationale)

Fig.9. Eadwine Psalter, self-portrait of the scribe (Cambridge, Trinity College, cod. 17.1, fol. 283v) (courtesy of the Master and Fellows of Trinity College, Cambridge)

Fig.10. Valerianus Gospels, Cross-colophon page (Munich, Bayerische Staatsbibliothek, Clm. 6224, fol. 202v) (courtesy of the Bayerische Staatsbibliothek)

Fig.11. Flavigny Gospels, Christ and Evangelists page (Autun, Bibliothèque Municipale, MS 4, fol. 8r) (courtesy of the Bibliothèque Municipale)

Fig.12. Jack Ziegler, drawing of writer with angelic inspiration (copyright The New Yorker Magazine, Inc.)

Fig.13. Hrabanus Maurus, *De laudibus sanctae crucis*, Monk kneeling before cross (Vienna, Österreichische Nationalbibliothek, cod. 652, fol. 33v) (courtesy Österreichische Nationalbibliothek)

Fig.14. Ostrogothic eagle fibula from Domagnano (courtesy of the National Museum, Nuremberg)

Fig.15. Codex Amiatinus, Prophet Ezra (Florence, Biblioteca Medicea-Laurenziana, cod. Amiatino 1, fol. Vr) (courtesy of the Biblioteca Medicea-Laurenziana)

Fig.16. Lindisfarne Gospels, Evangelist Matthew (London, British Library, cod. Cotton Nero D. IV, fol. 25v) (courtesy The British Library)

Fig.17. Sutton Hoo ship burial, hinged clasp (courtesy The British Museum)

Fig.18. Incredulity of Thomas, ivory from Echternach (courtesy Staatliche Museen Preussischer Kulturbesitz, Berlin)

Fig.19. Incredulity of Thomas, ivory from Constantinople (courtesy Dumbarton Oaks)

Fig.20. Crucifix, ivory from Trier (courtesy Schatkamer, Sint Servaaskerk, Maastricht)

Fig.21. Liuthard Gospels of Otto III, Emperor in Majesty (Aachen, Domschatz, fol. 16r) (Bildarchiv Foto Marburg)

Fig.22. Trier Gospels, Tetramorph (Trier, Domschatz, cod. 61, fol. 5v) (Rheinisches Bildarchiv)

Fig.23. Plan of St. Gall (St. Gall, Stiftsbibliothek, cod. 1092) (after Horn and Born, *The Plan of St. Gall* 1.xxvii [full ref. in Nees, "Originality," n.91], courtesy of The University of California Press)

Fig.24. Gian Lorenzo Bernini, Ecstasy of S. Teresa, Cornaro Chapel, S. Maria della Vittoria, Rome (Alinari)

Fig.25. St. Dunstan's Classbook, St. Dunstan kneeling before Christ (Oxford, Bodleian Library, cod. Auct. F.4.32, fol. 1r) (courtesy The Bodleian Library)

INTRODUCTION:

THE END OF THE 'DARK AGES'

CELIA M. CHAZELLE

The articles in this volume began as invited papers delivered at the conference, "A Symposium on Early Medieval Culture," held at Bryn Mawr
College with funding from The J. Paul Getty Trust, on April 8, 1989. In
keeping with the symposium's broad definition of the term, "culture," they
focus on a range of different types of records that early medieval people have
left us of their ideas, beliefs, and tastes. These include political documenta-
tion as well as religious, artistic, and literary source-materials, sources that
provide us with insights into the lives and thought not only of the intellectual, literate elite in the early medieval west but also, sometimes, into the
concerns of the illiterate mass of the population; for cultural endeavor, it
perhaps needs to be stressed, should not be considered something confined
to the literate.

The first article, by Seth Lerer, deals with the confrontation of orality
and literacy in Anglo-Saxon England. The point of departure is the story
of Imma in the *Ecclesiastical History of the English People,* the account of
England's conversion completed in 731 by the Northumbrian monk, Bede,
and the story's vernacular retellings in the Old English version of the *History*

as well as in Aelfric's homily on the glories of the Mass. One aim is to demonstrate how Bede and his Anglo-Saxon interpreters deliberately weighed certain aspects of Imma's story and manipulated its language in order to reshape it according to their own particular aims, among them the desire to express their Christian convictions as to the primacy of Christian texts and literacy over pagan orality. In the initial recounting of Imma's story Bede provides, as Lerer puts it, "a kind of parable of the mythologies of writing operating in a newly Christian Anglo-Saxon England." The story serves to ground both Bede's own authority as a writer and that of the Roman Church with its texts.

The second paper, by Thomas Noble, analyzes the years from c. 785 to 794 in the reign of Charlemagne (c. 742-814), the Frankish king and later emperor in the west, as the period in which the king and his advisors engaged in the careful elaboration and public implementation of a new "ethos of rulership" by which the Carolingian kingdom was to be governed, one centered on the Christian virtues of justice, humility, clemency, peace, and wisdom. This was expressed through some of the major state papers that the Carolingian court issued during those years, beginning with the loyalty oaths and *Admonitio Generalis* of 789 and moving on to the massive treatise known as the *Libri Carolini*, written in 790-793. The seemingly disparate issues confronted in these documents, ranging from educational reform to the iconodulism of the Byzantine Empire, Noble argues, mask the evidence they also provide of a more single-minded intentionality that helped dictate the form and contents of each text, so that they set forth the new ideology of western kingship based on Christian morality.

The third contribution to the volume, by Lawrence Nees, takes us into the sphere of art historical research on the early medieval west. Nees' interest is in the problem of "originality" in artistic production. Is the term ever applicable to surviving works of art from early medieval, western Europe? While other scholars have answered that question primarily in the negative, Nees contends that a significant number of artistic creations from this period and region do in fact deserve to be considered original in various respects. The readiness of scholars to deny this, he argues, owes much both to the current focus of medieval art historical research on the search for sources and to the clearly important role that models played in many early medieval works of art. For this reason, though, the indications also available that the creators of these works could try for novelty in "formal or stylistic arrangements, technical procedures, expression, subject matter, and function," and that they could consciously rearrange and alter the material that they borrowed from their models, have often been ignored. It is time, Nees contends, to give full due to the evidence here not only of the influence of models, but in addition of deliberate originality based on human initiative, and moreover of an originality that contemporaries held to be a factor adding to an artistic production's worth.

All three articles are indicative of the essentially more positive attitude towards the intellectual and cultural achievements of the early medieval west that has surfaced in scholarship of the past two decades. In addition to re-examining the extant evidence, such scholarship testifies to a rethinking, in several disciplines of the humanities, of older assumptions concerning the relative merits of early medieval western culture and its relationship to what was found in Antiquity and high medieval Europe. In this regard it is impor-tant to note at the outset, in light of what was said earlier about the nature of "culture," the emergence especially in the last ten years of a new sensitivity to the fact that culture is not synonymous with literacy, despite a tendency in older scholarship on medieval Europe to link the two.[1] In the early medieval period, by which is commonly meant the era in western European history stretching from approximately the fall of the last Roman emperor in 476 to the tenth or eleventh century,[2] the society that grew out of the confluence of ancient Mediterranean civilization with that of the so-called "barbarians" who moved into regions once controlled by the Roman Empire was one in which information was transmitted primarily through oral communication. Only a very tiny and very select minority of the population possessed the ability to read or to write. For the most part they were members of the clergy, since at least until the ninth century Latin was virtually the sole lan-guage used in a written form in the west. Yet many scholars now emphasize that the sparcity of literacy (Latin literacy) in this society should not obscure what it nonetheless achieved in terms of thought and cultural activity, as is discernible from the array of artifacts and even writings to survive from the period, some of which also preserve echoes of the vast oral culture that has otherwise been lost to us.[3]

As already suggested, most recent scholars who have focused on the cul-ture of the early medieval west, including the three contributors to this vol-ume, have diverged sharply from that older scholarship which preferred to write off the age as the nadir in the cultural development of western Europe. This preference was exemplified by the frequent references that such works contain to the "Dark Ages," whether the phrase was used to designate the entirety of the period or only a portion of it.[4] The epithet is one that has largely passed out of commission; where it still occurs in modern scholarship, it is usually employed with the understanding that what is dark about those centuries is principally our knowledge concerning them, hampered as it is by the paucity of extant writings and artifacts to inform us about life at the time.[5] Outside the range of specialists' studies of the period, though, one still occasionally encounters the older and different view that the shadows engulf-ing early medieval Europe were partly or wholly inherent to the era.[6] The darkness, from this perspective, is attributed to a widespread disintegration of civilizing forces in the west, caused by massive disruptions to antique civilization through the barbarian migrations into the region. As one account of early medieval Europe recently put it:

> At the time [late seventh century] the so-called Dark Ages stood probably at their darkest. The Roman Empire had been swept away forever by successive waves of barbaric tribes, who had conquered most of western Europe including northern Italy, much of which lay in the hands of the brutal Lombards. Pope Sergius I reigned over Christendom in a crumbling Rome, whose statues had been stolen or decapitated, and whose population had been reduced from over a million to thirty thousand or so. The Arabs marched on, subduing Spain and threatening France. East of the Rhine total savagery prevailed.[7]

Although this description does represent an extreme assessment of a small unit of time within the early Middle Ages, and was not written by a professional historian, it echoes views that up until the last two decades were expressed in numerous studies of the period as a whole. In all likelihood, it is a description based on readings in the large amount of this older literature that still circulates widely.[8]

An unfavorable regard for the general quality of life and thought in the early medieval west is most noticeable in scholarly work of the nineteenth and first half of the twentieth centuries. Implicitly or explicitly, those writings often evaluated the early Middle Ages via larger interpretations of western history from Antiquity through the Middle Ages that emphasized how on many points the early medieval centuries witnessed a divergence – generally regarded as a "decline" – from norms and standards of political, social, economic, and cultural (including intellectual) behavior that had existed in Antiquity, in some ways survived in the new Roman empire of Byzantium, and that to a certain extent resurfaced in the west later in the Middle Ages.[9] As these studies might stress, beginning in Antiquity and continuing through the early medieval period dramatic transformations happened on a number of levels in western European life. Among the changes to which reference was often made, in such contexts, were the penetration of barbarian groups into areas controlled by Rome, with the myriad consequences this had for the character of life in the ancient Roman Empire, along with the drop in population levels, the decline in trade, and the shift from a money economy to reliance more completely on barter as the norm of economic exchanges. During the early Middle Ages, as was also frequently observed, urban centers shrank or disappeared and communities became more self-sufficient, as the breakdown in the older lines of communication forced them to rely more fully on their own resources. Slavery, the principal source of agrarian man-power in the Roman Empire, was replaced in many areas by systems that settled peasant families on their own land. Western Europe evolved into a society whose focus was far more predominantly rural than it had been under the Roman Empire, with the manor, in regions controlled by the Carolingians, becoming a main economic, social, and administrative unit. In terms of cultural phenomena, the early medieval west turned in some ways away from the norms of classical education, and urban schools disappeared in which the laity might acquire thorough grounding in this type of education. In writing, as has often been noted, adherence to classical rules of Latin grammar, style, and spelling declined, and learning became more thoroughly oriented towards the teachings of the Christian Church, while the pursuit of knowledge in other areas was increasingly controlled by a regard for how that knowledge would improve mastery of Christian learning. With artistic endeavors one can notice, among other developments, greater indifference to the standards of illusionism found in ancient Roman painting, a new regard for forms and styles developed outside the sphere of Roman art, and a virtual disappearance of large-scale sculpture in the round.

The single, most significant interruption that was usually recognized to these patterns of change was the one that occurred during the century and half of rule in Francia by Charlemagne (c. 742-814), his son, and his grandsons. For historians who followed the work done by Henri Pirenne in the early part of the twentieth century, the Carolingian age marked the true beginning of the Middle Ages and of "Europe" itself.[10] Despite its perceived importance, however, the very sharpness of the interruption with previous centuries, as that interruption was understood, was taken to highlight the degree to which western civilization had altered since the fifth century. Furthermore, because the Carolingian Empire did not really last beyond the ninth century, it was set in contrast to the transformation of medieval culture and society that began in the eleventh century and from then on undercut the political, economic, and cultural structure of early medieval civilization. At this time there commenced new, steady and at certain points rapid growth in population that raised it even beyond the level seen under the late Roman Empire, the emergence of new technologies and more extensive, efficient agriculture that helped make the population growth possible, an increase in the size and importance of western cities, the formation of larger and more stable units of political and economic power, an increase in trade, a growing circulation of money and reliance on it in economic exchanges, a rise in the level of education among the clergy and also within the lay population, a new interest in and familiarity with classical, pagan learning that found its reflection not only in high medieval writings but also in art, a new precision to the vocabulary and organization of thought, the appearance of new centers of learning and of new centers of artistic production. Comparisons of western, early medieval Europe with early Byzantium only served to underscore still further the transformations that occurred in the west before the ninth century: thus attention was drawn, for instance, to the continuity of early Byzantine imperial government with that of the Roman Empire, to the more pronounced "classicizing" tendencies noticeable in early Byzantine art, the longer survival there of antique centers of education, the greater importance of Constantinople than of any western city as an urban center and focus of wealth, the higher level of education that eastern clergy could attain, in these centuries, or correspondingly to the more intense theological discourse in which they sometimes engaged.[11]

In general, where the focus was brought to bear on cultural developments, it can be argued that studies dealing with the early medieval west from the angles just described too readily perceived the confrontation of antique Mediterranean traditions with those of the Germanic groups which settled in western Europe, in Antiquity and the early Middle Ages, from the vantage-point of the obstacles this set to the continued spread and evolution of Roman culture and of a corresponding decline in that civilization.[12] To put it more bluntly, "civilization" was equated with classical culture; the diminishment of the latter was one and the same as the demise of the former. For the pre-Carolingian age, especially, less space was therefore allotted to investigating the situation from a more positive angle, one that, for example, highlighted the influx of new peoples carrying different ideas, artistic tastes, religious and political traditions, for which Roman culture gradually made room and to which it slowly adapted. Little discussion was also given to the potential of individuals who lived at the time to respond through writings and art, and also through oral forms of expression, to the changing world around them. Such studies frequently overlooked the possibility of active, creative energies in the early medieval west, of people who could be inspired by the new social, intellectual, and artistic crosscurrents to break deliberately away from old patterns and experiment with new combinations of ideas or new artistic formulae.[13] This seems all the more remarkable when one considers that "creativity" – with the willingness to change and to innovate that the word indicates – is far more likely to flourish in a predominantly oral environment than in a highly literate culture, which precisely because of its emphasis on written records tends to be conservative in outlook. (What is more conservative, for example, than American attitudes towards the written document of the Constitution?)

In keeping with the efforts of scholars now to break with these tendencies in older studies of the early medieval west, Lerer's examination of the story of Imma in Bede's *History* and in its later Anglo-Saxon versions, where Bede and his later interpreters each carefully crafted the story, in different ways, into an exposition of the confrontation of pagan orality with Roman, Christian literate culture, demonstrates how early medieval writers could exploit this intersection of cultural streams. Nees' article makes a similar point concerning early medieval artists, who, he shows, did not merely seek to adhere to the artistic traditions that came down to them and were not simply swept along by cultural developments entirely outside human control. Rather, again, it is often apparent that they consciously selected from the sources available to them, and, at times, invented for themselves new styles, patterns, and motifs, in part by reworking what they received from the past. Even though older scholarly literature traditionally set the Carolingian age apart from the rest of the early Middle Ages as a sort of hiatus in the general cultural decline, here, too, perhaps because of the overall low assessment of the centuries between Antiquity and the high medieval period, one finds places where the true character of certain developments and the initiative of individuals was not adequately appreciated. Thus Noble argues that past scholarship did not realize completely the significance of certain political events and writings from Charlemagne's reign in the 780s and early 790s in part because those years were too narrowly viewed through the prism of the imperial coronation in 800. His study of key documents from 785-794 reveals more clearly the scope, depth, and conscious intentionality these texts express, aiming toward the reform of society and its governance in conformity with Christian virtues.

In its writings and in its art both pre-Carolingian and Carolingian Europe left a record of how the confluence of values, tastes, traditions, and ideologies from the Mediterranean with those of the barbarians gradually resulted in a culture that owed something to all these forces yet, for this very reason, was unlike any previously seen in the western world. It was a culture that revealed to a striking degree the ability and willingness of individual writers, political leaders, and craftsmen to formulate new modes of thought, new styles, and new tastes from disparate sources, in order to cope with the changing cultural climate in which they found themselves. While this is a facet of early medieval history that is now receiving increasing consideration,[14] much work clearly remains to be done. Even with the progress that has occurred in research in the field, it is possible to suggest that the entire significance and impressiveness of some of these achievements have yet to receive all the recognition they are owed, while in many cases inadequate scholarly resources mean that the remains of early medieval culture have not yet been studied carefully enough to ascertain their importance. Gatherings such as the Bryn Mawr symposium and the publication of papers such as those delivered at the conference will assist the progress of the other research that is now moving in this direction, it is hoped, both by shedding further light on specific instances of cultural endeavor in the early medieval west and, more broadly, by encouraging greater scholarly interest in the period.

The older tendency to downgrade the culture that arose from the inter-section of Germanic with Roman-Christian traditions, in the early medieval west, and the slow pace at which some elements of the cultural achievement of the era have come to be appreciated, can partly be traced to a few, long-standing obstacles to any attempt to look closely at the period. Among them, mention should be made first simply of the continued paucity of sur-viving writings and other artifacts from the era, despite the improvements here through recent archaeological research.[15] The scarcity of material ev-idence makes it hard for any historian who tries to analyze the texts and other objects that have been preserved to understand the conditions under which they arose, as is necessary, in fact, in order to grasp their full signifi-cance. Even the proper date or provenance to assign a given artifact can be notoriously up in the air, which clearly poses problems for any other kind of research touching on it.[16] Beyond this, however, the scarcity of materials perhaps leads us, still today, to be more startled than we should be by the sophisticated nature of some of the writings and artifacts from that time. Although this does not pose a problem in the study of ancient Greco-Roman civilization, when one turns to the early Middle Ages it seems to encourage treatment of those artifacts that are extant less as indications of a culture to a large extent now lost to us, than as pinpoints of light emphasizing the darkness of their surroundings. The very rarity of surviving materials, a rarity that cannot be taken as a thorough measure of what the society and its people in fact produced, may itself promote a more negative perception of early medieval, western culture than it deserves.

Additional difficulties arise from traditional boundaries between aca-demic disciplines, which still make it uncommon to find scholars of one dis-cipline who are truly conversant with another. When dealing with a period such as the early Middle Ages from which so little has come down to us, though, the place that a particular text or artifact such as a work of art or a political document held in the development of its surrounding culture may not be sufficiently understood without reference to information gleaned through other avenues of research. Still another problem connected more precisely with the study of texts is the willingness of some scholars, even occasionally today though more noticeably in previous decades, to accept without question the opinions of early medieval writers who described their task not as to develop ideas of their own but merely to preserve and trans-mit the thought of their predecessors. Particularly in older scholarship, these writings were regularly dismissed as derivative, unoriginal, and representa-tive of a general decline since Antiquity in intellectual accomplishment.[17] Such judgments were especially severe when the writings in question quoted or paraphrased at length from earlier authors, as do many works from this period. Such low regard for these works may have been connected with twentieth-century antipathies towards plagiarism, the implicit conclusion being that the texts in question were to be judged according to this modern notion. They were also doubtless influenced by an overly rosy idea of the "originality" and "creativity" of modern cultural production, which tends to forget that today as in earlier ages the best artists as well as writers seek inspiration and borrow from earlier sources. One result is that too little serious attention was paid to the often highly creative fashion in which early medieval writers and also artists could develop on and thus move beyond their sources (as Nees and Lerer demonstrate in their articles). By choosing carefully from among earlier texts and images, arranging the portions chosen with other materials, altering words and motifs, otherwise reshaping the borrowed materials, and joining them to elements of their own creation, people of the early medieval west could express what were often very different ideas from any their sources were intended to convey.[18]

Finally, the study of early medieval, western culture has in the past been obstructed by certain preconceived, intellectual frameworks for interpretation of the history of western civilization. Outside of any actual evaluation of cultural achievements in the early medieval west, these strongly encouraged a negative appraisal of the period relative to perceptions of western culture in other centuries. Three such structures of thought may be isolated for mention here.[19] The first is an overly rigid respect for the periodization schemes that have been traditionally employed in surveying past centuries. As Noble shows in his article, periodization is valid insofar as it serves to break down the past into smaller units of time that are more accessible to historical research. These units may then be investigated, for example across the boundaries between traditional academic concerns, in ways that can reveal historical currents binding together otherwise seemingly disjointed events – as Noble shows is true regarding key Carolingian documents from the 780s and early 790s. In dealing with the broad sweep of developments from Antiquity through the Middle Ages and into the Renaissance, however, the effort to find the boundary between the beginnings of medieval Europe and the end of Antiquity, or between the end of the early Middle Ages and the beginnings of the high medieval period, has regularly led to greater consideration for the differences between these eras (whatever the centuries assigned to them) than for the continuities that also exist. The differences that are there cannot be ignored or underrated, yet both sides of the picture clearly must be kept in mind.

Second, growing out of the work of Italian Renaissance humanists, there is the tendency to glorify Antiquity, on the one hand, and on the other hand the movements to recover the literary, artistic, and intellectual heritage of Antiquity as representative of the high-points in cultural achievement. For

Renaissance thinkers, the Middle Ages constituted an age of barbarism that deserved their scorn (despite their admission of improvements in the high medieval period) because it supposedly had not sought, as they did, to rediscover the values of ancient Rome and had not looked to classical literature, thought, and art for inspiration. Since the Renaissance, but drawing partly on medieval writers' views of the aims of their own times, the western appreciation for cultures that seem consciously to emulate the culture of the ancient Mediterranean has been used to isolate periods within the western Middle Ages when some level of similar interest in the re-appropriation of classical culture can also be discerned. Among the periods most often identified in this manner are the Carolingian renaissance, the Ottonian, and the renaissance of the twelfth century. Such epochs have therefore been the focus of most research on the cultural evolution of medieval Europe, and within this context attention has centered on their distinctiveness as new movements to imitate or absorb the learning of Antiquity – their distinctiveness, above all, from the years before and after the "renaissances" are determined to have occurred. Ironically, these eras have been praised both as the highpoints in cultural creativity in the west and for their imitation of classical culture, with often little attempt to understand how in them the processes of creation and imitation came together. Not only does all this mean, once more, that the continuities between preceding or subsequent years and the identified periods of renaissance have received proportionally less notice than have the points on which they can be differentiated. In their own right, even today, the centuries in which the medieval west is not recognized to have produced a renaissance more rarely arrive at the center stage of research, and hence are more rarely the subjects of close, careful analysis.

For the early medieval period this has had two consequences: At least for continental Europe, the stretch of centuries between the fifth and the late eighth remains the longest without any identified renaissance.[20] Except where attention has been directed to Anglo-Saxon culture and its ramifications on the continent, these centuries have generally inspired less interest in their cultural development than has, for instance, the Carolingian era. And furthermore, as far as the Carolingian renaissance from the late eighth through the ninth century is concerned, the focus on the ways in which Carolingian writers and artists collected, borrowed from, and imitated ancient works, styles, and techniques has added to the tendency to interpret their efforts as motivated mainly or even solely by the desire to preserve and transmit the heritage of Antiquity. In the last two decades scholars who examine the Carolingian period have largely avoided abandoning the concept of renaissance, and in fact their work has shown that rejection of the term would in certain ways be wrong.[21] But the same work has also looked more critically at the nature of the movement involved in the eighth and ninth centuries, apart from any predetermined notions of renaissance based on other movements in western history. Thus it has stressed how, beyond the preservation of antique culture, the Carolingians could also deliberately rework and transform that heritage and add to it in ways of their own making, to accord with their particular social, political, and cultural needs.

History has also sometimes been viewed as inherently cyclical, or perhaps better, "organic," and this is another model of interpretation that has affected how the early Middle Ages have been perceived. The idea is one that has been traced back to Greek and Roman historians.[22] When applied in twentieth-century scholarship to the study of the west, following the boundaries between eras formed in efforts to periodicize western history,[23] the span of time reaching from before Greek and Roman Antiquity to our day has been viewed as a series of cultures following one upon the other, each of them moving from birth through a process of maturization, to a peak of cultural achievement, and then entering a period of decline that leads to its demise – its death – before another civilization can arise (be born) to take its place and undergo a similar evolution. The civilizations of ancient Rome and of the Middle Ages constitute two such cycles, then, with the decline of the former coming principally in the fourth and fifth centuries, and ending with Rome's fall or in the few centuries thereafter, of the latter in the centuries leading up to the Protestant Reformation. Here again the early medieval west must necessarily be understood as a lowpoint in western civilization, whether it is placed at the ebb of the cycle started in Antiquity or at the beginning of a new one.[24] In either case it leads away from the previous summit of antique culture, and it at best commences the "upward" movement that culminated in the high Middle Ages.

As was indicated beforehand, the efforts by scholars today to reassess the character and significance of the western early Middle Ages, including its cultural achievements, have helped take scholarship away from the negative impact of these models of interpretation and of the other obstacles noted to study of the period. Studies of early medieval society as a whole together with those more specifically of its literature, politics, theology, or art[25] have made us more aware of the high quality of many writings and artistic productions to have survived from the early medieval west, and have thrown important light on their significance by rethinking their relationship with other, contemporary developments. Even the former distrust of the early medieval reliance on sources, in written work and in artistic imagery, has begun to be set aside in favor of greater understanding for the innovative manner in which sources could be handled by writers and artists of the era. These results have been assisted by insights gleaned through archaeological studies, as well as by the new interest in comprehending the significance of the dominant orality of the Middle Ages and its interaction with the slowly emerging literacy.[26] They have also been helped by awareness of the need to cross the boundaries between traditional disciplines in order to shed greater light on the accomplishments that occurred in each. And they have been aided, too, by recognition of the prejudices concerning the early medieval period that still survive, partly because of our preconceived notions about the course of western civilization from Antiquity through the Middle Ages.

From such research on the culture of the early medieval west has developed a greater appreciation for the roles of early medieval writers, artists, political leaders, and others not only in the preservation of remnants of other civilizations, but in shaping their varied heritage, often actively, consciously, and intelligently, to suit their own needs in confronting very new conditions of life. The three articles included in this volume are contributions to this effort to form a clearer, more accurate picture of the aspirations and concerns that determined how the culture of the early medieval west took form, as well as of that culture's breadth.

Notes

* I am grateful to Professor Emmet McLaughlin of Villanova University for comments and criticisms that have helped me in the preparation of this introduction.

1. This is a basic assumption, e.g., in the literature that characterizes the early Middle Ages as the "Dark Ages": see below, n.4. Cf. Robert Hoyt, ed., *Life and Thought in the Early Middle Ages* (Minneapolis, 1967), 3-6. It must be stressed that I make no attempt whatsoever here to survey the immense scholarship on the early Middle Ages or even a particular portion of it. Rather, the following notes mention only a handful of scholarly works which, I think, are representative of the themes and issues to which I refer. Those studies indicated are mainly works in English or English translation, since it is to these that readers of this volume are most likely to have access. Particularly useful bibliographies found in some of this literature are also noted.

2. To name but a few of the countless synthetic treatments of the Middle Ages or the early medieval period that have used this time-frame or one close to it: Charles Oman, *The Dark Ages, 476-918*, 5th ed. (London, 1908); Margaret Deanesley, *A History of Early Medieval Europe, 476-911*, History of Medieval and Modern Europe 1 (London, 1956); H. St. L.B. Moss, *The Birth of the Middle Ages, 395-814* (Oxford, 1935), e.g. v-vii, where the beginning of the Middle Ages is dated to the death of Theodosius; David Nichols, *The Medieval West, 400-1450: A Preindustrial Civilization* (Homewood, Ill., 1973); Warren Hollister, *Medieval Europe: A Short History*, 4th ed. (New York, 1978); R.H.C. Davis, *A History of Medieval Europe, From Constantine to Saint Louis*, 2nd ed. (London, 1988). Cf. Jean Hubert, et al., *Europe of the Invasions*, The Arts of Mankind (New York, 1969), with extensive bibliography of earlier art historical literature on the early medieval west. Other works may employ a different periodization scheme where the influence of the Pirenne thesis can sometimes be noticed, such that the Middle Ages are considered to begin only with Charlemagne's reign or with his imperial coronation: e.g. (arguing that this is the proper interpretation for art historians), John Beckwith, *Early Medieval Art*, Praeger World of Art Series (New York, 1964), 9. Cf., with reference to other literature, Judith Herrin, *The Formation of Christendom*, (Princeton, 1987), 295. Cf. also David Herlihy, ed., *Medieval Culture and Society* (New York, 1968), xii. For a modification of Pirenne's thesis, Richard Hodges and David Whitehouse, *Mohammed, Charlemagne, and the Origins of Europe: Archaeology and the Pirenne Thesis* (Ithaca, N.Y., 1983). Other scholars opt for other points of departure, depending on the particular geographical areas and issues with which they deal: e.g., in regard to England, Doris Mary Stenton, *English*

Society in the Early Middle Ages (1066-1307), 4th ed. (Harmondsworth, 1965).

Concerning the impact of Pirenne's thesis on determinations of when the Middle Ages began, see Richard E. Sullivan, "The Carolingian Age: Reflections on Its Place in the History of the Middle Ages," *Speculum* 64 (1989): 267-306, at 269f. and n.9.

3. On the confrontation of orality with literacy in the Middle Ages and our knowledge of the nature of the oral culture, see e.g. the works mentioned in n.26, but especially Brian Stock, *The Implications of Literacy: Written Language and Models of Interpretation in the Eleventh and Twelfth Centuries* (Princeton, 1983).

4. E.g. Oman, *The Dark Ages* (above, n.2); C.W. Previt-Orton, *A Shorter Cambridge Medieval History* 1 (Cambridge, 1962), e.g. 283; Davis, *History*, Part 1: "The Dark Ages" (above, n.2); Hugh Trevor-Roper, *The Rise of Christian Europe* (London, 1965), esp. 23f.; David Talbot-Rice, ed., *The Dark Ages: The Making of European Civilization* (London, 1965). Cf. Herlihy, ed., *Medieval Culture and Society*, xii (above, n.2).

5. E.g. Peter Brown, "A Dark-Age Crisis: Aspects of the Iconoclastic Controversy," in idem, *Society and the Holy in Late Antiquity* (Berkeley, 1982), 251-301, see again 263f. Also printed in *English Historical Review* 88 (1973): 1-34. F.W. Maitland held that the period was dark not because of immorality but because it was difficult to understand: see Giles Constable, "The Study of Monastic History Today," in Vaclav Mudroch and G.S. Couse, eds., *Essays on the Reconstruction of Medieval History* (Montreal, 1974), 19-51, at 22. It has been noted, too, that the early Middle Ages are dark only relative to later periods (not to earlier ones); "Gaul and Britain in the sixth century or the ninth are far better known to us than at any time during the Roman period." Edward James, *The Origins of France: From Clovis to the Capetians, 500-1000* (New York, 1982), 6. James goes on to claim that, in terms of our knowledge of history, "With the early Middle Ages, in fact north-western Europe is emerging for the first time from its 'Dark Ages'."

6. An example of an extreme version of the older attitude is a statement by Ferdinand Lot concerning the tenth century, of which James takes note: "The tenth century is truly sterile. It is one of those periods of which one can say that it would have been better if it had never existed." James, *Origins*, 6; F. Lot, *Naissance de la France*, rev.ed. (Paris, 1970), 483.

7. Frank Delaney, *A Walk in the Dark Ages* (London, 1988), editor's summary (jacket). Cf. p. 89.

8. The notions of a Middle Age and a Dark Age were originally synonymous, taking shape in Renaissance and post-Renaissance literature. Both referred

to the whole of the period from late Antiquity to the beginning of the Italian Renaissance. Attitudes towards the early part of the Middle Ages comparable to that expressed in the passage quoted above, even if they tend to be expressed in more restrained language, are found in much older scholarship, e.g. some of the works cited in n.4. See also (referring to other literature where such attitudes are evident), Hodges and Whitehouse, *Origins of Europe,* 3 (above, n.2); Hoyt, *Life and Thought,* 8 (above, n.1).

9. See e.g. the literature written before 1960 cited above in nn.2, 4, and the discussion of traditional assessments of the different "periods" of the Middle Ages in Norman Cantor, *Medieval History: The Life and Death of a Civilization,* 2nd ed. (London, 1969), 10-12. R.W. Southern (*Western Society and the Church in the Middle Ages,* The Pelican History of the Church 2 (Harmondsworth, 1970), 24) wrote: "The fall of the Roman Empire left a mental and spiritual as well as a political ruin which it took centuries to repair. The collapse was a long and complicated business, but in the West it was complete by the end of the seventh century. It was then that the work of rebuilding began...."

10. Cf. Sullivan, "The Carolingian Age," 270.

11. This is evident for instance from the complex doctrinal debates of the great ecumenical councils of the period, which were all held in the eastern empire and were attended almost exclusively by eastern churchmen. For overviews of the developments just outlined see e.g. Herlihy, ed., *Medieval Culture,* 1-19, and the older works of Deanesley, *Early Medieval Europe*; R.F. Arragon, *The Transition from the Ancient to the Medieval World,* The Berkshire Studies in European History (New York, 1936), e.g. 85ff.; Joseph R. Strayer, *Western Europe in the Middle Ages: A Short History* (New York, 1955); J.R. Strayer and Dana C. Munro, *The Middle Ages, 395-1500,* The Century Historical Series (New York, 1942), cf. esp. 95.

12. See e.g. with regard especially to early medieval thought, George E. McCracken, ed., *Early Medieval Theology,* The Library of Christian Classics 9 (Philadelphia, 1957), 15; David Nichols, *Medieval West,* 26f., 30 (above, n.2). Cf. Emile Amann, *L'Epoque carolingienne,* Histoire de l'Eglise 6 (Paris, 1947), esp. 14ff. (referring to the pre-Carolingian situation). In relation to artistic achievement e.g. Arnold Hauser, *The Social History of Art* 1 (New York, 1951), e.g. 147: "After the barbarian invasions a new society arose in the West with a new aristocracy and a new cultural elite. But whilst this was developing, culture sank to a low-water mark unknown in classical Antiquity and remained unproductive for centuries...."

13. Caecilia Davis-Weyer has remarked, against this trend in earlier scholarship, "To maintain some degree of cultural unity in a time of such turbulent and radical change required the unremitting efforts of patrons, artists and

intellectuals, who had to gain their own sense of historical continuity by sub-
mitting to what must have been an often painful process of education and
transformation. The paucity of early medieval records tends to give a false
air of impersonality to the art of this period, making us forget how very large
a role individual choice and initiative had to play in its making." In idem,
ed., *Early Medieval Art, 300-1150,* Medieval Academy Reprints for Teaching
(Toronto, 1986; first published by Prentice-Hall in 1971 in the series Sources
and Documents, ed. H.W. Janson), ix.

14. E.g. in recent monographic studies of individuals, specific institutions,
writings, and artifacts from the early Middle Ages, too numerous to list here
(though see those mentioned in the notes to the articles in this volume). Reference should also be made to the work of Peter Brown, most accessible in
the collections of his articles on the east and the west in late Antiquity: *The
Making of Late Antiquity* (Cambridge, MA, 1978); *Religion and Society in
the Age of St. Augustine* (New York, 1972); *The Cult of the Saints: Its Rise
and Function in Latin Christianity* (Chicago, 1980); *Society and the Holy in
Late Antiquity* (above, n.5). See also the excellent, recent work by Patrick
Geary, *Before France and Germany: The Creation and Transformation of
the Merovingian World* (New York, 1988), with bibliography; Herrin, *The
Formation of Christendom* (above, n.2); Josef Fleckenstein, *Early Medieval
Germany,* trans. Bernard S. Smith, Europe in the Middle Ages, Selected
Studies 16 (Amsterdam, 1978), with bibliography; J.M. Wallace-Hadrill, *The
Frankish Church,* Oxford History of the Christian Church (Oxford, 1983),
with bibliography. See also James, *Origins* (above, n.5), with bibliography.
Cf. Lawrence Nees' illuminating introduction to his *A Tainted Mantle: Her-
cules and the Classical Tradition at the Carolingian Court,* The Middle Ages
(Philadelphia, 1991), 3-17.

Making good use of new scholarship for his account of the early Middle
Ages is Edward Peters, *Europe and the Middle Ages* (Englewood Cliffs, NJ,
1983). Three important, recent collections of essays are, Patrick Wormald,
et al., eds., *Ideal and Reality in Frankish and Anglo-Saxon Society: Studies
Presented to J.M. Wallace-Hadrill* (Oxford, 1983); Janet Nelson, *Politics and
Ritual in Early Medieval Europe* (London, 1986); and Thomas F.X. Noble
and John J. Contreni, eds., *Religion, Culture, and Society in the Early Middle
Ages: Studies in Honor of Richard E. Sullivan* (Kalamazoo, Michigan, 1987).

15. See Philip Dixon, *Barbarian Europe* (New York, 1976); Hodges and
Whitehouse, *Origins of Europe* (above, n.2). As Geary has noted, the evidence provided by archaeologists "... is the only source for understanding
the non-literate world of barbarian society not filtered through the language,
and thus the categories, of Greco-Roman culture." Geary, *Before France and
Germany,* vii (above, n.14).

16. Cf. Wayne Dynes, "Tradition and Innovation in Medieval Art," in James M. Powell, ed., *Medieval Studies: An Introduction* (Syracuse, N.Y., 1976), 313-342, at 331f.

17. To offer only one paradigmatic example here, McCracken, ed., *Early Medieval Theology* (above, n.12), 15: "This was a time when men thought much less of the originality of their own productive genius than of the preservation in an age of turmoil of the values transmitted to them in mysticism and morality out of the Christian past. Their attitude towards this inheritance was loyalty to its admittedly high standards, rather than a self-centered conviction that it was their privilege, much less their duty, to develop the faith in novel directions." While it is quite true that this was the attitude early medieval churchmen typically expressed towards their authorities, too often it has led to the conclusion that their writings in fact contain no ideas original to them.

18. For an early medieval usage, e.g., of a passage by Augustine that deviates sharply from the way Augustine meant it to be read, see C. Chazelle, "Pictures, Books, and the Illiterate: Pope Gregory I's Letters to Serenus of Marseilles," *Word & Image* 6 (1990): 138-153.

19. Cf. Stock, *The Implications of Literacy,* 5; Geary, *Before France and Germany,* vi-vii; N. Cantor, "The Interpretation of Medieval History," in *Reconstruction of Medieval History,* ed. Mudroch and Crouse (above, n.5), 1-8; Dynes, "Tradition and Innovation," esp. 329-339 (above, n.16).

20. This is true despite the watering-down of the notion through overuse: cf. John J. Contreni, "Carolingian Biblical Studies," in Uta-Renate Blumenthal, ed., *Carolingian Essays: Andrew W. Mellon Lectures in Early Christian Studies* (Washington, D.C., 1983), 71-98, at 71.

21. See esp. Janet Nelson, "On the Limits of the Carolingian Renaissance," in idem, *Politics and Ritual* (above, n.14), 49f. For an extensive bibliography of early and recent literature on the Carolingian age, as well as for a discussion of the process of its definition over the years, see Sullivan, "The Carolingian Age" (above, n. 2). See also Donald A. Bullough, "*Europae Pater*: Charlemagne and his Achievement in the Light of Recent Scholarship," *English Historical Review* 85 (1970): 59-105.

22. See e.g. Robin G. Collingwood, *The Idea of History* (Oxford, 1946); Cantor, "Interpretation of Medieval History," 3f.

23. E.g. Strayer, *Western Europe,* 9 (above n.11), where Strayer argues that the whole medieval period constitutes one "cycle" in history, covering the rise and fall of a single civilization; in such cases one sees, he declares, "... how peoples of the past slowly became capable of organizing and integrating their efforts, how they accomplished their great and characteristic work, how they

eventually lost their ability to do constructive work and slipped into stagnant and retrogressive activities...."

24. The two choices reflect the impact of Pirenne's thesis on the study of the early medieval west. See above, n.2.

25. As above, n.14. See also the work by the three scholars represented in this volume: Seth Lerer, *Literacy and Power in Anglo-Saxon Literature* (Lincoln, NE, 1991); Thomas F.X. Noble, *The Republic of St. Peter: The Birth of the Papal State, 680-825,* The Middle Ages (Philadelphia, 1984); Lawrence Nees, *The Gundohinus Gospels,* Medieval Academy Books 95 (Cambridge, MA, 1987); idem, *A Tainted Mantle* (above, n.14).

26. E.g. Franz Bäuml, "Varieties and Consequences of Medieval Literacy and Illiteracy," *Speculum* 55 (1980): 237-265; Stock, *Implications of Literacy* (above, n.3); Rosamond McKitterick, *The Carolingians and the Written Word* (Cambridge, 1989); idem, ed., *The Uses of Literacy in Early Medieval Europe* (Cambridge, 1990). Cf. Lerer, *Literacy and Power* (above, n.25). In relation to problems in medieval art, see Herbert L. Kessler, "Pictorial Narrative and Church Mission in Sixth-Century Gaul," in *Pictorial Narrative in Antiquity and the Middle Ages,* ed. H.L. Kessler and Marianna Shreve Simpson, Studies in the History of Art 16 (Washington, D.C., 1985), 75-91; Michael Camille, "Seeing and Reading: Some Visual Implications of Medieval Literacy and Illiteracy," *Art History* 8 (1985): 26-49.

LITERATE AUTHORITY IN BEDE'S STORY OF IMMA

SETH LERER

Readers of Bede's *Ecclesiastical History* will remember the chapter in Book 4 which tells the story of Imma, a thane who was taken prisoner after the battle between kings Egfrid and Ethelred and yet who could not be bound by his captors. Whenever he was tied up, the bonds became loose and fell from his body, and Bede attributes this miraculous action to the prayers of Imma's brother, a priest named Tunna. Thinking his brother dead, Tunna offers masses for his soul, and with each recitation of the Mass, Imma's bonds fall away. Upon his eventual release, Imma returns to his town, finds his brother, and learns the true reason for the apparent marvel.[1] At one level, Bede explicitly offers this story as an exemplum on the power of prayer and the efficacy of faith. It must have been one of the more appealing of his capsule biographies, and three centuries after its composition, Aelfric retold it in a homily on the glories of the Mass.[2] But at another level, this is a story about popular superstition and Christian understanding, and about the proper role of texts and ritual in transmitting that understanding. To modern readers, it is as puzzling as it is well-known, and what has puzzled them most is precisely that relationship between text and superstition that Bede foregrounds in the tale. Bede's explanation of the miraculous loosening of Imma's bonds seems straightforward enough, but not so that of Imma's captor. For upon seeing the fetters fall away, the captor asks whether Imma "had about him any loosening spells *(litteras solutorias)* such as are described in stories *(fabulae)*" *(EH* 402-3), and with this question, the captor poses an interpretive dilemma for Bede's later Anglo-Saxon readers, as well as for his twentieth-century scholars.

Most modern readings of this passage have approached it from primarily philological and archaeological interests. Do these *litteras solutorias* refer to charms or spells, or to the letters of a written document or inscribed amulet? Little help is provided by Bede's Old English translator, who renders the phrase as *alysendlican rune,* the releasing rune(s); or from Aelfric, who rephrases the question in terms of sorcery and runology; or from scholars of the past century, who have adduced the passage and its translations as evidence for surviving Germanic magical practice in Bede's day or for magical runic inscriptions in a later Wessex.[3] "The search for Anglo-Saxon paganism" still informs research on this episode, even though no Old English charm for releasing fetters has been found, and though the status of rune-magic in pre-Conquest England has been irrevocably called into doubt.[4]

My purpose here will be to approach Bede's story of Imma from a different set of critical, literary, and historical perspectives. I read his chapter as a kind of parable of the mythologies of writing operating in a newly Christian Anglo-Saxon England. In its distinctions between history and fable, faith and superstition, runes and the Roman alphabet, releasing letters and the word of God, Bede's story dramatizes a fundamental break in the interpretive continuum from pre- to post-Conversion England. This is an exemplary moment in the *Ecclesiastical History,* one whose study, I will argue, may inform us of Bede's governing sense of a theory of signification and of his attitudes towards the literary uses of the Germanic past. It may also tell us something of Bede's treatment of authority in history writing and of the variety of ways in which he represents himself as the author of a written text and as the reader of his culture's documented past.

To clarify my exposition, let me state that I come to the chapter, and to the *History* as a whole, from three interrelated directions. First, I am concerned with how Bede represents the runic writing and the drama of signification in the story. The experience of Imma and his captor illustrates the confrontation of the individual with an alien or cryptic form of writing. In these terms, the difference between Christian and pagan in the *Ecclesiastical History* may be considered as much one of signs as of belief. A credence in charms or spells signals a reliance on the power of the signs themselves, on something of a "word magic" which a later readership would associate with runic writing. But for the Christian, the sign is a symbol, a representation of the divine will. Such symbols may function within a larger system of rite and ritual, a system such as the Mass itself, whose power comes not from any signs or actions per se, but rather from its symbolic reenactment of the spiritual typologies which govern Christian living. It is in the interest of a converting Church, though, to perpetuate a notion that its converts once believed in a nonsymbolic magic of the letter. Whatever the historical threats of a resurgent paganism, the imagined re-creation of this earlier, pre-Christian world is central to the Church's institutional success. By telling exemplary stories of the power of the Mass, Bede and later Aelfric reaffirm the power of the Church's rites, and in so doing, make explicit claims for the need for its historians and writers.[5]

Miracles and their retellings are perhaps the most palpable – and indeed the most controversial – of such articulations of that power. Much has been made of the function of miracles in the *Ecclesiastical History,* and even more has been said about the notion of the miraculous in early medieval life in general.[6] Here, the miraculous nature of Imma's release takes shape against the foil of pagan superstition voiced by his captor. His sense of incomprehending wonder contrasts with the sureness of Bede's own faith in the miracle. For Bede, the miraculous is intimately linked with the processes of history writing: with the *historia* he transcribes, not the *fabula* which transmits knowledge of the charm. The self-conscious reflections on the written nature of the work and on the ways in which writing transforms received legend into doctrine come to distinguish the miraculous from the merely marvelous. The distinction between the captor's knowledge of magic as a species of fable and Bede's own work as a history reaffirms the place of texts in the religious narrative. By relegating a knowledge of the releasing letters to the realm of oral lore, Bede privileges his written narrative, garnering for it an *auctoritas* similar to those texts which form the basis of a monastic education. His purpose, as I intend to show, lies in acculturating early legend into the literate and literary structures of a Christian knowledge, be they those of saint's life, institutionalized prayer, or written history. My reading of this chapter, and by implication of the *Ecclesiastical History* as a whole, seeks to unfold his arguments for practical and spiritual literacy by showing how he simultaneously invents and supresses details of pre-Conversion systems of interpretation.

Bede's relationship to the Germanic past, and his construction of his own authorial persona through this fable of a runic text, finds its analogy two chapters after Imma comes home, when the cowherd Caedmon leaves the feast to find the inspiration to produce the first Old English Christian poem. Bede's story of Caedmon, perhaps the most famous of his narratives, has rightly become one of the canonical texts for the study and teaching of Old English.[7] But it has become so precisely because it seems to affirm those nineteenth- and twentieth-century cultural notions of the oral nature of archaic literature and the spontaneity of poetic performance. Caedmon's Hymn has long been taken as a paradigm for the synthesis of Christian doctrine with heroic diction seen to motivate much of Old English poetry, and Caedmon himself has been taken as a model for the scop who populates the narratives of *Beowulf,* the reminiscences of *Widsith,* and the laments of *Deor.* My second critical direction, therefore, is to realign the study of Caedmon by situating it in the narrative trajectory of Book 4 of the *Ecclesiastical History.* What is at stake here, I argue, is the way Bede transforms old Germanic myths of poetry as drink and inspiration into a new Christian literate environment. Bede puts Caedmon in a scene of literary eating and drinking only to remove him from it and to posit a new kind of "alimentary" poetics: a poetics based, now, on the *ruminatio* of a monastic education. In the course of Bede's account, Caedmon changes from an unnamed cowherd to a named poet, from a public performer to a private meditator, from a secular individual to a member of a religious community. Caedmon's life traces the argument for poetry as textual and for the origins of English literary history in the canons of religious study. Much like his story of Imma, Bede's chapter on Caedmon illustrates his transformations of the old mythic imagination into the institutions of the literate life.

Imma and Caedmon can also help me make a point of theory and method. Scholarly assumptions for the primacy of Caedmon's story may be understood as part of what Derrida had identified as the traditional western understanding of the primacy of speech over writing. Derrida's critiques of the mythologies of writing, and the theoretical positions they have generated, call attention to an almost natural suspicion of the absent and the written. In the scholarship which has grown up around the Caedmon story, and in the debates about the "orality" of early English verse, we may also find a version of this need to see the spoken as not only chronologically anterior to writing, but also as somehow better, more original, or truer to the essence of the literature.[8] This problem of a scholarly ideology provides the third direction for my study, namely, the translation and reception of Imma's story by later Anglo-Saxon readers. The Old English version of the *Ecclesiastical History* and Aelfric's homily on the efficacy of the Mass constitute sustained, critical reworkings of Bede's idiom and method. For lack of a better term, they may function as examples of a "literary criticism" designed to revise and rephrase a canonical historical text for a new interpretive readership. While the Latin historian suppresses or elides discussion of the details of a pagan practice, his vernacular transmitters reinvest their terminology with words of ancient and Germanic resonance. In Aelfric's homily and throughout the Old English Bede, the references to runic writing will be used in what we may think of as a literary or imaginative way. Their phrasings turn the stories of Imma, and I will suggest of the conversion itself, into a literary legend rather than a piece of history. They distance the events of the *Ecclesiastical History* from a contemporary Anglo-Saxon audience, making them transpire in a deep past rich with magic or with ritual. In a similar way, the vernacular version of the Caedmon story brings out the embedded legends of a mead of poetry, and in turn, of the distinctions between the new Christian literate community and the old oral world of performance.

The study of past texts also involves the making of canons, and whether for the modern scholar or the Anglo-Saxon homilist, canons and their maintenance are central to the learning of the past. Aelfric affirms the place of Bede in the traditions of a literate education, and his homilies effectively create a syllabus of study for the believing reader. By drawing on some recent reassessments of the social function of canons and canonicity, I hope to draw out some of the principles by which Aelfric rewrote Bede's story of Imma and considered it a part of the documentary evidence for miracles and mysteries. His injunction at the close of his homily to read Gregory is thus a charge to augment his spoken arguments with independent written confirmation, and in these terms we may say that notions of belief here structure themselves through forms of reading. Whether in the syllabus of study enjoined by Aelfric, or the sequence of scriptural writings which will form the outline of a Caedmonian poetic project, or the list of Bede's own works which closes the *Ecclesiastical History,* canons of texts give shape to a new Christian understanding of the world. The creation of such canons dovetails, therefore, with a notion of interpretation which sees signs as symbols, where the power of the word comes not from any sorcery of the incision, but from the correctly acted rites of God and his Church.

i.

I begin, then, with the deep past. When Imma's captor asks about the releasing letters he conjures up a vision of Germanic magic, and while there are no extant Old English charms to support the currency of such a spell, there is a Continental tradition for the magic of release. In the Old High German First Merseburg Charm and in the Old Norse myths of Odinn we may find the analogues to Bede's releasing letters.[9]

> Eiris sazun idisi   sazun hera duoder
> suma hapt beheptidun   suma heri lezidun
> suma clubodun   umbi cuoniouuidi
> insprinc haptbandun   inuar uigandun.

> (Once the women were settling down here and there. Some were fastening fetters, others were hindering the host, others were picking apart the fetters: escape the bonds of captivity, flee from the foe.)

At the heart of the First Merseburg Charm is not simply the imagery of binding and loosening, but the strong pagan context of its composition and the distinctive military coloring of its diction. The *idisi* who sit wrapping and unwrapping the fetters descend, perhaps, from the prophetic women of ancient Germanic society described by Tacitus. Their survivals may be found, in Old English, in the *ides* who works the spells of *dyrne cræft* in the Cotton Maxims, and they are clearly cousins to the Old Norse *Herfjotur,* one of the Valkyrie goddesses who assist Odinn.[10] These "warrior-fetter" women, as Georges Dumézil and Helen Damico have illustrated, personify the god's power over armies, a power rendered in the First Merseburg Charm in the phrase, "suma heri lezidun." This detail resonates, as well, with another Old Norse analogue in the *Brot af Sigurðarkviðu* (ch.16), where Brynhild, cursing Gunnar after Sigurd's murder, dreams that he would ride "cheerless, fettered into the enemy army."[11]

These details in the Charm, and their potential Old Norse analogues, yoke together a collection of allusions to the myths of Odinn. In the *Hávamál,* and in his later appearances in Snorri's *Ynglingasaga,* Odinn appears as a master of runic writing, the worker of spells, and the emblem of a dark wisdom. Long associated with the story of Imma are these lines from the *Hávamál,* where Odinn catalogues his magic arts, and where, in particular, he announces his charm *(lioð)* for releasing bonds.

>   Þat kann ek hit fiórða,   ef mér fyrðar bera
>   bond at boglimom:
>   svá ek gel,   at ek ganga má,
>   sprettr mér af fótom fioturr,
>   en af hondom hapt. (*Hávamál* stanza 149)

(This fourth one I know. If men fetter my limbs, I chant such a charm as will let me escape. The fetter flies from my legs, the handcuff from my wrists.)

Synthesizing this information with other Eddic material, Snorri states that Odinn taught his various skills "with runes and songs which are called charms *(galdrar).*"[12] Among his many spells, he knew those which could open up the mountains, rocks, and burial mounds: "and with words only he bound up those who dwelled in them" ("ok batt han með orðum einum pá, er fyrir bjoggu," *Ynglingasaga* 19). It is the power of such words alone which marks the force of Odin's magic, for it is through his mastery of runes, charms, and songs that the god extends his power over land and people. For Snorri, his status as a master of such "word magic" differentiates him from the pantheon of other powerful or guileful deities.

The place of this early Germanic material in the study of Bede's story of Imma is, then, less a question of source study than a matter of comparative mythography. Their shared interest in the appearance of magic on the field of battle, and in the idioms of bondage and release, word and symbol, may say much about the uses of the pagan past in newly Christianized societies and about the distinctions between magic and miracle in times of social strife.[13] The act of writing down the two Merseburg Charms, according to

Susan Fuller, bespeaks a possible lapse into pagan belief in the face of brutal invasion and political disunity in tenth-century Saxony. As such, they represent the unique transcription of an orally transmitted, popular poetry, rather than the continued rescription of a pre-existing text. Snorri's encyclopedic transmission of Norse mythology, by contrast, attempts to catalogue the subjects and the techniques of a vernacular poetics for a Christian readership.[14] But unlike these potential analogues, who preserve their mythological information for Christian readers in relatively complete form, Bede's account of the releasing letters is fragmentary and allusive. He seems to care neither for the wording of the spell nor for its historical context, and I would argue that Bede remains deliberately vague on the specifics of this magic not because he wishes to deny the details of forbidden craft, but rather because he needs only to evoke in the reader's mind the impressions of a superstitious belief.

Bede's goal, in brief, is transformation rather than preservation. His concern lies with the representation of the Germanic past in a Christian present, and with the need to suppress or mediate the details of that past within the symbolic structures of Christian narrative. The *fabulae* behind the releasing letters offer a case of pagan, oral lore juxtaposed against a Christian, written *historia*. They show us, in the captor's question, an adherence to a way of thinking characteristic of an earlier, Germanic past – a credence in the power of the *littera* itself. To translate it into Snorri's later, but apposite terms, Imma's imprisoner imagines something of an Odinnic force, a power to bind and release "með orðum einum," with words alone. But for Bede, the power of the Mass and the power of his story lie in their shared symbolic force: their parallel transcendence of the mere words or letters which convey them. The story of Imma, in this sense, is thus deeply typological, its pattern shaped by the narrative conventions of a literary hagiography. The confrontation of the spiritual man with disbelieving captors becomes a narrative trope pressed into the larger structures of bondage and release, exile and homecoming. Imma's story recapitulates the larger patterns of the soul's spiritual release from sin, as the thane's request from King Hlothere for ransom money *(redemptionis)* echoes the familiar conceptions of Christ buying back mankind with his death. As Irenaeus of Lyons put it, developing what would become an influential passage for later thinkers, Christ "gave himself as ransom *(redemptionis)* for those who were led into captivity."[15] Led out of captivity, released and returned, Imma reenacts the basic narrative moves which govern the literature of holy men, and by this observation I do not mean to imply that Imma is himself a saint, or that Bede seeks to conceive of the thane's actions as inherently holy. Rather, I mean to make a point of literary form: that Bede transforms this story of a marvel into the exemplum of a miracle; that by reworking Imma's experience into the literary form of a saint's life, he makes the story mean more than it says.[16]

His chapter now exemplifies the place of the symbolic for a Christian reader-ship. It casts human experience into a Christian, literary form, a form which grants symbolic meaning to a story not bounded by the letters of his own text. *Historia,* then, differs from fable not only in its written form; it differs fundamentally both from the fable and the *litteras solutorias* in that its written narrative encompasses symbolic meaning. Such meaning, in the end, is granted to it by the reader's awareness of an inherent literary structure – a structure explicated not by the author but by the audience itself.

Bede's vagueness on the magic, then, is not the product of a bad memory but an act of literary suppression. These charms do not survive within the story on the written page, nor should they live within the conscious memory of a Christian audience. They exist, if they exist at all, purely in the world of rumor or of lore. They remain simply in the *fabulae* of a superstitious world, and in this manner, the *litteras solutorias* stand for all forms of groundless belief. Imma's story replaces the supposed efficacy of these charms with the true power of the Mass, and in so doing, replaces popular stories of the marvels of words with Bede's own document of faith.[17] That faith finds its expression in the commentary on Imma's return to his homeland. The thane's narration of the events of capture and release, together with the details of Tunna's intercession, instill in the hearing populace a new faith in the power of God. Bede's own voice then takes over, and concludes the chapter by noting that he himself heard this story from reliable witnesses, and by stating that he will now commit it to writing within the scope of the *History.*

> Hanc mihi historiam etiam quidam eorum, qui ab ipso uiro in quo facta est audiere, narrant; unde eam quia liquido conperi, indubitanter historiae nostrae ecclesiasticae inserendam credidi.

> (This story was told to me by some of those who heard it from the very man to whom these things happened; therefore, since I had so clear an account of the incident, I thought that it should undoubtedly be inserted into this *History.*) (*EH* 404-5)

Bede implicitly contrasts oral narrative with written text, and points towards a difference in the responses of a listening audience and a reading public. His strategy is two-fold. First, by associating himself with the audience – placing himself as a listener at the story's telling – Bede situates himself within the lived time of narrative performance, asserting in turn both the veracity of his informants and the authority of his own writing. Second, he enshrines the story within that writing, turning from tale to text and thus preserving it for future readers. He renders judgment on the tale, finding it credible and its inclusion in the *History* indubitable, as its narrative facts conform to an implied set of criteria for inclusion. What Colgrave and Mynors render as the clear *(liquido)* account of this report can in addition be considered as its uninterrupted or unadulterated narrative typology: it is a perfect story for the *History* precisely because it conforms to the consistent forms of storytelling found throughout its chapters. At stake in Imma's tale is not simply its miraculous events; rather, it is its resonance with narratives of spiritual life and its reliance on the confrontation between believer and unbeliever in terms of signs.

That confrontation, and Bede's reflections on its import, find a striking parallel earlier in the *Ecclesiastical History,* in Book 1 chapter 25, when Augustine and his missionaries, newly arrived in England, confront King Aethelberht. Dubious of their mission, and unsure of his own response, the king refuses to meet Augustine in any enclosed building, "for he held the traditional superstition that if they practiced any magic art, they might deceive him and get the better of him as soon as he entered."[18] In a manner similar to that of Imma's captors, Aethelberht gives voice to a misapprehension basic to the argument of the *Ecclesiastical History:* the mistaking of miracles for sorcery by the unbelieving or the ill-informed. Mired in old beliefs, the king at this point can grant the missionaries only hospitality, and Bede makes explicit here – in a way no longer necessary by Book 4 – the basis of this misapprehension: "But they [the missionaries] came endowed with divine, not devilish power and bearing as their standard a silver cross and the image of our Lord and Saviour painted on a panel."[19] The force of this assertion, and its relevance to Imma's story, lies with the interpretation of incised signs. The distinction between divine and devilish craft – that is, between the power which informs miracles and the trickery which only seems marvelous – finds its symbolic representation in the cross and painted panel which the missionaries bear. Such representations are not to be found in the charms or amulets implicitly present in the king's fear and explicit in Imma's captor's question. The cross and panel function *as* amulets, as Christian replacements for the older, pagan talismen which would have been the expected accoutrements for one learned in the *maleficae artis.* These now are symbols of power, rather than embodiments of power in themselves, and Bede's Old English translator, I think, recognized these multiple resonances between the two events.

His vernacular brings out the imagery of charms embedded in Aethelberht's response by shifting the focus of sorcery in the confrontation. In the translation it is Aethelberht who uses an old charm to work against Augustine's supposed sorcery: "breac ealdre healsunge, gif he hwylcne drycræft hæfden" (Miller 58). The signs the missionaries bear similarly take on the status of a charm, as the picture of the Lord is "afægde 7 awritene" (colored and inscribed). These words, together with the reference to *healsung* and to *drycræft* hearken back to ancient pairings of **faihian* and **writan* in runic epigraphy, and in so doing, realign the context for Augustine's arrival.[20] At one level, the use of this Germanic idiom rephrases Christian iconography in traditional terms. Put simply, it deploys a familiar, vernacular vocabulary to describe an imported object. But at another, deeper level, the Old English translator says something about his own imagination of an early English past. The terms for magic craft and charms, for coloring and cutting, invest this scene with a distinctively "runic" quality: they make both Aethelberht's fears and Augustine's appearance somehow strange and ancient, much as the idioms of runic writing make the scene with Imma's captor dense with magical allusions. There, the imprisoner asks "hwæðer he ða alysendlecan rune cuðe, 7 þa stafas mid him awritene hæfde" (Miller 342). The written staves of the captor's imagination recall the supposed charms and incised portraiture of the encounter between Augustine and the king. But instead of a rune, it is a *healsunge* which the king deploys; what is *awritene* in Thanet are not the *stafas* of a spell but the *tacn* of the Lord. Read in juxtaposition, what these two English episodes announce is that the power of the sign lies in the mind of the unbelieving beholder: that while the loosening of the bonds may seem a work of magic *stafas,* Imma and the reader know it to be the work of God's word; that while the king may see only the picture of the Lord, we are invited to go beyond the coloring and the cutting to see the *tacn* – the symbol or the "token" – of salvation.

Both episodes thus dramatize the encounter between the traditions of an oral lore and the authority of God's word. They offer explorations of a Christian literacy, where texts are to be taken for their deeper symbolic or typological value, and where it is the purpose of the learned to interpret and to explicate them beyond the literal. Such explorations fill the *Ecclesiastical History,* as Bede textualizes its key events. In the chapters on the conversion which follow those on Aethelberht, for example, Bede narrates the mission in terms of its texts, reproducing Gregory's letters verbatim and dramatizing the exchange of documents which mark Augustine's bishopric. It is against this grounding of the new religion in writing that Aethelberht's superstitions must eventually be rejected. Again, and in an analogous manner, Bede follows Imma's story with the chapters on Hild and Caedmon, pointedly illustrating the power of the new Christian, vernacular poetry to absorb written doctrine. In this context, the argument of the Caedmon story concerns not so much what it tells us of oral composition, but what it tells us of Bede's own agenda.

ii.

Here, as elsewhere, Bede takes Germanic oral forms and grounds them in texts, and Caedmon's story may be read as a narrative of the Christian literate appropriation of an earlier poetics. The Old Norse legends of the origin of poetry, with their attentions to the mead of Odinn and the sacrificial aspects of its preparation, share a common Indo-European ancestry with the great myths of Sanskrit, Avestan, and Old Irish traditions.[21] Central to these many treatments is the communal act of drinking and the ritualized environment in which the liquid – be it soma, mead, or kvass – is produced and ingested. Central, too, is a relationship between the liquid and the human or divine body, and summarizing much of this material in his own distinctive way, Georges Dumézil considered what he called the "ideologies of insobriety" to be among the earliest and most pervasive of the Indo-European social myths (*Gods* 23). In particular, he located the accounts of literary drinking and ingestion in those moments when, through social strife and reconciliation, opposing classes, factions, or systems of belief come together. In myth, he found such moments in the "pledge of peace" which led the Norse gods to spit into the same bowl and eventually give rise to Kvasir. In what he thought of as social history, he found such moments in the coming together of sorcerer-priest and hunter-warrior groups. Now, while Dumézil's researches have been challenged by more recent Indo-Europeanists, I think his characterization of this pattern offers a still useful guide to certain literary archetypes, and in particular, to Caedmon's story. The common pattern to these stories exists, Dumézil wrote,

> at the moment when divine society is with difficulty but definitively joined by the adjunction of the representatives of fecundity and prosperity to those of sovereignty and force, [and] it is at the moment when two hostile groups make their peace that a character is artificially created incarnating the force of intoxicating drink or insobriety and is named after it. (*Gods* 23)

Drawing out the archetypal narrative embedded here, we may say that the nexus of drink and poetry appears at moments in which social strife and reconciliation are dramatized. From this engagement, there emerges a figure who is christened by name as the poet, and who establishes a new relationship both to the drink and to the culture. Caedmon's naming and his appearance in Bede's story may conform to these broad outlines. His departure from the feast, inspiration in the cow-shed, and entry into the monastery chart a progressive synthesis of two contrasting cultures. He himself comes to embody the traditions of both sacred and secular, social and monastic. Read more specifically in Dumézil's terms, Caedmon straddles the worlds of those who represent fecundity and prosperity (i.e., the cowherds, farmers, or other providers who participate in the feast) and those who represent sovereignty and force (i.e., the Church and its members, and the monastic community which owns the land on which Caedmon and his peers had worked). His visit to the reeve and his introduction to the abbess dramatize this move from those who serve and provide to those who rule. Caedmon's *Hymn* itself will join these two groups. In its verbal transformation of religious history into heroic diction, the poem, as it were, "makes peace" with two opposing ideologies, and it is at this moment that the poet is himself "created."

Read in this manner, Bede's story of Caedmon both conforms to and rejects the old myths of the origin of poetry. Like many traditional accounts, Caedmon's naming represents the sanctioning of the poet or poetic figure by specially empowered authorities. In the story of Finn MacCoul, for example, the young hero is transformed into a poet through the eating of the cooked salmon and the sucking of his burned thumb. Allusively combining references to sacred food and spittle, this moment in the "Boyhood Exploits of Finn" announces that "whenever he put his thumb into his mouth, and sang through *teinn laida* [illumination of song?], then whatever he had been ignorant of would be revealed to him" (Meyer 186). The new poet is then renamed, "Finn is thy name, my lad." The narrator continues, "It is then Finn made this lay to prove his poetry" (Meyer 186). Much like the Irish poet's performance of his lay – a pastoral of Creation – Caedmon, newly named, sings his own hymn of Creation to "prove his poetry" to himself and his angel. But if Caedmon's story may be likened to a myth, it is most unlike the many other stories of heroic saints and saintly heroes Bede himself had told in the *Ecclesiastical History*. Bede does not begin, as he had begun so many of these stories, by naming Caedmon himself. Instead of an expected introduction in the manner of "There was a monk named Caedmon," all we find is the story of a nameless *frater quidam*. We know who Caedmon is precisely at the moment when he has absented himself from the feasting, and in this narrative deferral, Bede transforms the traditional mythology of poetic naming buried in the scene. What we find is a poet who is not part of the earlier traditions, a poet who receives his gift not from the drink but from God. This is no story of the mead of poetry, as Snorri might have it, nor is it the same kind of account as that embedded in the Finn story. This is a legend of a poetry without the drink, a story of poetic origins stripped of the structure and the imagery of the *gebeorscipe*.

If Bede strips the origins of English poetry from its ancient mythology of drink, he replaces it with a different kind of ingestion. After he enters the monastery, all Caedmon's subsequent poetic works are products not of spontaneous effusion, but of *ruminatio*. As Bede puts it:

> He learned all he could by listening to them [i.e., the monks] and then, memorizing it and ruminating over it, like some clean animal chewing the cud, he turned it into the most melodious verse.

> (At ipse cuncta, quae audiendo discere poterat, rememorando secum, et quasi mundum animal ruminando, in carmen dulcissimum conuertebat....) (*EH* 418-19)

Here, the cowherd who had fed the cows becomes himself a proper rumi-
nator when he moves from shed to monastery. Unlike his earlier miraculous
performance – and unlike the impressions of his achievement garnered by
most modern scholars – Caedmon's later poetry comes not from sudden inspiration but from study. It comes not from the voice of angels but from the
mouths of men. And it comes not in the dreamt solitude of the cow-shed,
but in the alert community of brethren. Caedmon's poetic corpus, Bede tells
us, speaks to and is a product of the rightful rumination on divine texts.

Bede had commented extensively on rumination in monastic life, and his
remarks, as André Crépin recently has illustrated, rely on an inheritance of
commentary from Jerome, Augustine, and the many allegorical interpreters
of Mosaic law concerning cud-chewing, "clean" animals. Perhaps the most
pointed of these earlier accounts is Augustine's:[22]

> For it is by this very rumination, the mark given by God, of clean
> animals that God has meant that anybody must swallow what he
> hears into his heart so that he should not be idle while thinking
> over it, but, when listening, he should resemble someone eating, and
> then, when he summons what he has heard back to his memory and
> recalls it in a most sweet meditation, he should resemble a chewing
> creature.

This passage had been quoted and discussed in Crépin's argument on
Bede and the monastic life, and Crépin too has noticed Caedmon's act of
rumination in its institutional context. But what he does not follow out are
the specific resonances between Augustine's remarks and Bede's narrative.
As a "chewing creature," Caedmon offers the sweetest verse *(carmen dul-
cissimum)*, and the sweetness of this poetry echoes the "sweet meditation"
which, in Augustine's words, accompanies the act of remembrance ("cogita-
tione dulcissima recolit"). The verse, in turn, sounds "so sweet" *(suauiusque)*
that his teachers become his listeners, and the Old English translator, in a
frequently discussed departure from the Latin, brings out the implications
of this ruminative poetics.

Bede had simply stated that the poet's words sounded so sweet that his
own teachers had become his listeners ("suauiusque resonando doctores suos
vicissim auditores sui faciebat"). But the Old English version of this scene
vivifies the metaphor embedded in monastic *ruminatio* and illuminates the
nature of the place of poetry in the religious community.

> Ond his song and his leoð wæron swa wynsumu to *gehyranne* þætte
> selfan þa his lareowas *æt his muðe wreoton ond leornodon.* (Miller
> 346).

(And his song and his poetry were so joyful to hear, that his very own teachers wrote down and learned from his mouth.)

While the Latin makes the teachers the listeners, the Old English makes the listeners the writers. In putting down and learning Caedmon's poetry, these monks bring vernacular verse into the scribal culture of monastic learning and its transmission. What they hear from his mouth becomes the new object of the process of *ruminatio*. The Old English verbal sequence "gehyran, writan, leornian" matches precisely the directives to the Benedictine monk – to hear, transcribe, and memorize or learn – and in tracing out the processes of study, Bede's vernacular translator shows these teachers as ruminating creatures themselves. As the objects of that rumination, therefore, Caedmon's poetry from this point on will have its origin and afterlife in books. He makes his verses out of Genesis, defined in the Old English as "seo æreste Moyses booc," and out of "þaes halgan gewrites canones boca" (a phrase which expands on Bede's "sacrae scripturae historiis"; Miller 346; *EH* 420-21). This version of a textualized Caedmon, too, returns us to the opening of Bede's chapter, where we are told, in the Old English, that he learned "of godcundum stafum þurh boceras geleornode" (rendering "ex diuinis litteris per interpretes," Miller 342; *EH* 416-17).[23]

At moments such as these, Bede's Old English translator brings out both the ancient and contemporary resonances of the *Ecclesiastical History*'s stories. Just as he had made explicit the runic flavor of Imma's "charm" or of Augustine's signs, so he recalls the legends of the drink of poetry by turning Caedmon's *conuiuio* into a *gebeorscipe* (beer-drinking party). In addition, he invigorates the metaphor of *ruminatio* with a specific reference to the actions of the poet's *mud* and with detailed attention to the scholarly activities of his monastic teachers. In what becomes effectively a reading of the Caedmon story, the Old English translation makes explicit Bede's association of the origins of English poetry – and in turn of English literary authorship – with the conventions of monastic reading. It becomes a story, much like that of Imma, which reflects on Bede's own status as an author and transmitter of received tales. It reflects, too, on Bede's and his translator's status as translators, as they both testify, directly or implicitly, to the difficulties of rendering vernacular verse in Latin prose, or of transforming Latin prose into Old English diction. They, like Caedmon himself, become figures of *ruminatio*, as they bring the old Germanic idiom into the lettered world of Christian understanding.

Read in sequence, the chapters of Imma and Caedmon juxtapose a Germanic past with a Christian present. Both represent that past in terms of myths or dreams of language, whether they be the imaginations of a runic magic or the visions of a bardic verse. When placed into their Christian present, these accounts will ground themselves in the reading and writing of texts, and more pointedly, in the proper performance of the sacraments. Both stories hinge on the correct interpretation of a sacramental act. Tunna's performance of the Mass and Caedmon's last request for the Eucharist, of course, make statements of doctrinal importance for Bede and his audience. They also make a literary statement, as they function in the patterns of romance typology which govern both narrations. For Imma, it is the progress of capture, bondage, release, and homecoming. For Caedmon, it is the sequential movement between outside public spaces and interior private enclosures. The sequences of inward movement match the patterns of ingestion which define the poet's life, and the chapter's close makes Caedmon's mouth once more the organ of his holiness. From his departure from the feast, through his entry into a monastic world of rumination, to the final taking of the sacrament, Caedmon's story sacralizes the old myths of eating, drinking, and poetic or prophetic knowledge.

Read in the ways I am suggesting here, we might say that the chapters on Imma and Caedmon present parables about the *Ecclesiastical History* itself. Taken together, they argue in fabulous or mythically-charged ways for the institutional authority of the Roman Church and its rites *and* for the literary authority of Bede's own narrative persona. They remind us, by the end of Book 4, that Augustine's judgments, Bede's reliable voice, or even Christ's power will find themselves articulated in the documents, letters, and codified practices of the Church. By the time we reach this moment in the *History,* we can recognize the *litteras solutorias* for what they are: a false textualization of a power which survives only in myth and fable. Writing is the province of Christian belief, and the miraculous is to be found in the workings of God's word and in the recognition that it needs a scripture or a history to document that power. As an oral narrative, Imma's life can awe and amaze, but only as a text can it affirm authority. Analogously, Caedmon's one spontaneous performance may please a supernatural listener, but only as transcribed and studied texts can the poetic canon of his making teach the human reader. In these terms, the miraculous power of the Mass or the symbolic quality of the Eucharist need to be understood not as popular beliefs but as learned, institutionalized practices. What I take to be Bede's supression of the specifics of pagan magic or his rejection of the old conception of a "liquid poetry" are, in their effects, repressions of the pagan modes of understanding. In a world denied the possibility of runic magic or an Odinnic mead of poetry, miracles must suffice, and Bede's purpose will be to find a place for the miraculous in a society now stripped of sorcery or superstition. His stories affirm God's power as the only supernatural instrument of change. Charms or magic formulae can hold no such control, for now, by relegating such things to hearsay or fable, Bede eliminates the vestiges of unbelief from the operative realm of the *Ecclesiastical History. Credidi* – I believed, and with this last word of

the story of Imma, Bede presents himself as a model of belief for a believing
readership.

iii.

Throughout the course of this essay I have apposed the Latin and Old
English versions of Bede's phrasing to suggest how the vernacular version of
the *Ecclesiastical History* offers a critical reading or literary interpretation
of the original. In Aelfric's homily on the efficacy of the Mass we may find
a fully formed rereading of Bede's Imma, one which draws perhaps on both
the Latin and Old English sources. Much like the translation of the *History*
itself, this homily may tell us much about the text's reception in a later
Anglo-Saxon England; about the notions that a West-Saxon readership had
about the legends of Bede's north; and about the hold that Imma's story
had on English readers as an imaginative re-creation of a Germanic runic
past for a Christian audience.

To a reader of Aelfric's homily, the story of Imma which it embeds may
seem but a pared-down version of Bede's tale. Imma is wounded, seized,
bound and ultimately released when his captor's bindings fail; again, when
he is sold into slavery, the impossibility of enchaining him provokes Imma's
ransom and leads to his return and reunion with his brother. Imma's ex-
planations for his freedom and his faith in the Mass appear relatively un-
problematic; and yet, the details of Aelfric's narration and the larger context
of his interpretation challenge any preconception that this is simply an un-
mediated retelling. Aelfric gets many of Bede's details wrong, a symptom
of what some have taken to be haste or confusion in his reproduction of the
History's chapter. Imma fights for the wrong side and is thus captured by the
wrong forces. The names and places Bede records are absent from Aelfric's
account: gone are the mentions of Tunnaceaster, named after Tunna, or of
King Hlothere, nephew of Queen Etheldreda, who provides Imma's ransom
money. Aelfric's phrasing of the captor's question in terms of sorcery and
runes, moreover, has suggested that a runic practice was alive in the Wessex
of the year 1000, or at the very least, that Aelfric had read the Alfredian
translation of the *Ecclesiastical History* and that he drew upon its idioms of
runes and staves for his own version of the captor's query:

þa axode se ealdorman þone hæftling, hwæðer he ðurh drycræft
oððe ðurh runstafum his bendas tobræce?

(The ealdorman then asked the captive whether he broke his bonds
through witchcraft or runestaves.) (*Sermones* 2:358-59)

Finally, Aelfric seems to care little for the interpretation of Imma's release, eschewing Bede's characteristic meditation on its import and reception, and preferring instead to end his homily with a brusque injunction to read Gregory for similar exempla.

Such "errors" or revisions say less about Aelfric's habits of composition or his knowledge of pagan ritual than they do about his literary interests and his work's controlling themes. Aelfric strips away historical detail to render Imma's tale into an exemplum rather than a chronicle. Its events transpire, here, in the deep past, and in Aelfric's handling they take on the status of a literary legend. It is an age of sorcery and runes, a vision of an earlier time as he imagines it. As such, it contrasts palpably with the world in which Aelfric and his audience now live: a world of books and schools, a world of English in the Roman, rather than the runic alphabet. Aelfric's reading of Bede's story fits into his larger interest in texts not just as objects of study or vehicles for communication, but as metaphors for social and political relationships. His conception of a vernacular literacy will differ from Bede's, and in consequence, so will his notion of the text, its authorship, and its integrity.

Throughout the Catholic Homilies Aelfric relies on written sources for his exempla, attending to their documentary status and the literate abilities required of their interpreters. The Bible and its commentaries, and the works of Jerome, Augustine, and Gregory all contribute to his explication of God's works and will. The centrality of texts to this project is clear, for example, in an Easter sermon on Christ's journey to Emmaus. Beginning with a claim for the necessity of learned instruction (2:283), Aelfric builds a pattern of quotations and allusions to the Gospels and to Gregory. References to the study of holy writ dovetail with quotations from written authorities (2:287). Christ "opened to [his disciples] the holy writings," and by this, Aelfric states:

> we magon tocnawan þæt us is twyfeald neod on boclicum gewritum. Anfeald neod us is, þæt we þa boclian lare mid carfullum mode smeagan; oðer þæt we hi to weorcum awendan.

> (We may know that we have a twofold need in bookwritings. Our simple need is to consider with an attentive mind the written teaching; the other, to turn it into works.) (2:284-85)

Texts, and in particular sacred texts, become the fundamental authorities for action and belief. The processes of reading and understanding motivate religious reflection, and for Aelfric, they form the basis for the structure of his own written sermons. Writing, too, affirms institutional authority, for not only does its mastery define the influence of scripture and its commentators, it defines that of contemporary priests and bishops. It is the bishop's duty to "instruct his people with book-learning" (2:320-1), and in the process, re-create the role of Christ himself as a teacher. In more metaphorical terms, literacy characterizes the relationships of priest and layman, man and God, man and king, as for example when he states that the true love of God internalizes all writings (2:314), or when he compares disobedience to God with a refusal to acknowledge the authority of the King's *gewrit*.[24]

Throughout these various remarks, Aelfric concerns himself with the proper uses of writing, and much like Bede, he focuses on the institutional structures through which writing grants power. To return to his version of Imma, we may now see those institutions at work in the interpretation of the story. For what Aelfric does here is not simply recast the plot, but resituate it in a canon of learned documents. Even before he gets to the thane's narra-tive, Aelfric attends to the experience of reading and writing which will mark both his own engagement with his source and the drama of interpretation offered in Bede's chapter.

> We rædað gehwær on halgum gewritum þæt seo halige mæsse mic-clum fremige ægðer ge ðam lybbendum ge ðam forðfarenum swa swa Beda, se snotera lareow, awrat on Historia Anglorum be sumu ðegene....
>
> (We read in many places in holy writings that the holy man greatly benefits both the living and the departed, as Bede, the wise doctor, has written in the *Historia Anglorum* of a certain thane....) (2:356-57)

At the outset, Aelfric situates Imma's story in the context of literate interpretation. The power of the Mass is to be understood through a partic-ipation in its glories and a reading of its miracles, as Bede himself becomes the authoritative chronicler of the role of the sacrament in English history. Through these opening moves, Aelfric shifts the focus of the narrative away from the popular experience of lore and roots it securely in the habits of study. *His* story of Imma is not the fresh transcription of an orally received account; it is instead the rescription of a canonical document of faith.

Aelfric's conclusion to the homily affirms the story's canonicity. His closing injunction to read Gregory the Great's *Dialogues* for similar exam-ples effectively brackets Imma's tale with allusions to *auctores* who embody written, Christian culture.

> Eac se halga papa Gregorius awrat on ðære bec Dialogorum hu micclum seo halige mæsse manegum fremode. Seo boc is on Englisc awend, on ðære mæg gehwa be ðison genihtsumlice gehyran, seðe hi oferraedan wile.

(The holy pope Gregory also has written in the book of Dialogues how greatly the holy Mass has benefited many. This book is turned into English in which everyone may hear abundantly on this subject, who will read it over.)(2:358-59)

Beginning with the text of Bede ("Beda... awrat") and ending with the writings of Gregory ("Gregorius awrat") he firmly situates the homily in the agenda of his own literary production and his claims for a vernacular readership. The instruction offered in this narrative, then, is one not only in the institutions of the Church and the power of its rites. It is as well an education in the power of its texts. It seeks to turn its audience into readers themselves: to make them informed interpreters of holy writ and religious history; to turn them away from *drycræft* and from runes and to the documentary inscriptions Aelfric and his sources exemplify.

Along these lines, we may return as well to Imma's captor's question and the status of the runes in Aelfric's homily. The similarity of his account to that of the Old English Bede has led most modern readers to assume a direct borrowing from the translation. But unlike Bede or his translator, Aelfric does not qualify the status of the runestaves or the sorcery as the subject of popular fable, and we might justly ask where he received his knowledge of the script. I would suggest that Aelfric learned about *runstafas* and *drycræft* in the same way he learned about religious doctrine or world history: from texts. In this case, it would be from documents of Old English poetry, and perhaps the poem which is the most similar to Aelfric in its phrasing here is *Andreas*.

Long dismissed as a late, derivative, or woefully doctrinal translation, *Andreas* nonetheless preserves a rhetoric of sorcery and runes strikingly apposite to Imma's story, and in fact, the very qualities about the poem which have marked it as distinctively late or unoriginal make it all the more appropriate as a source for the homilist's diction.[25] From its initial presentation of Matthew as the writer of the Gospel, *Andreas* shapes its heroes and its villains through the kinds of literacy they practice. In contrast to Matthew's ability "wordum writan wundorcræfte" (13), the cannibal Mermedonians who capture him will mark the death days of their captives through a form of writing "on rune and on rimcræfte" (134). Unlike that of the saints, or by implication of the *Andreas*-poet himself, Mermedonian writing attempts to bind and destroy rather than release and revive. Their inscriptions emblemize a pernicious kind of letter, one that literally kills, and the thematic function of such a misguided literacy finds its drama in the poet's later turn to an analogous group of villains. In the episode of the speaking stone, we see misreaders, rather than miswriters, in the personae of the unbelievers at the Temple of Jerusalem. These figures greet God's word only with superstition and distrust. Instead of receiving the *haliges lare* which the stone

offers (709-10), they remain mired in what had earlier been identified as the
deofles larum (611). Instead of learning the truths of this prophetic speech,
they simply and intuitively translate it into their own limited terms: terms
which, like those of Imma's captor, are those of sorcery.

> Ða ða yldestan   eft ongunnon
> secgan synfulle   (soð ne oncneowan),
> þæt hit *drycræftum*   gedon wære
> scingelacum,   þæt se scyna stan
> mælde for mannum....
>   þær was orcnawe
> þurh teoncwide   tweogende mod,
> mæcga misgehygd   *morðre bewunden.* (763-72)

(Then the wicked elders began afterwards to say [they did not recognize the truth] that this event was done through magical arts,
through devilish enchantments, that the beautiful stone spoke before the people.... There the doubting mind was evident on account
of their rebuke, the men's perverse thought, enwrapped in evil.)

The disbelievers effectively transform the clear words of God into *drycræft.*
They cannot see the *soð* in the *soðcwid,* and they respond not with the unity
of faith but with the duplicity of superstition *(tweogende mod).* Finally,
they become captives of their own doubt, bound here not in the real fetters of the Mermedonian's prison, but in the figurative bonds of spiritual
death *(morðre bewunden).* In revealing their ignorance, and in transforming
miracle into magic, the disbelievers offer a structural counterweight to the
Mermedonians and their captives. In both scenes, we may find the contrast
between virtuous and vicious forms of writing and interpretation. Whether
it be through "rune ond rimcræft" or through *drycræftum* and *scingelacum,*
magic practice or the credence in its spells are associated with the antitypes
of Christian heroism. By thinking in these terms, I suggest, Aelfric's version
of Imma's captor renders himself a figure on a par with those who "soð ne
oncneowan." Though he has tried to bind his captive he remains, within
this literary typology, the one bound in ignorance. He shares with the poetic
villains the apparent need to attribute God's miracles to sorcery, and this
affiliation gives to Imma's life the flavor of a literary parable. Shorn of its
historical details, phrased in the language of poetic magic, and bracketed as
a received document of faith, Aelfric's story of Imma functions no longer as
a chapter from Bede but as a free-standing, spiritual text.

Perhaps more than any single set of idioms or allusions, what affiliates
Aelfric's homily and *Andreas,* and what distinguishes them from Bede, is
what Erich Auerbach identified as the legendary style and its notable difference from historical narrative. "It is easy," he asserted in *Mimesis,* "to

separate the historical from the legendary in general," and he enumerates
the features of that separation:

> Even where the legendary does not immediately betray itself by
> elements of the miraculous, by the repetition of well-known standard
> motives, typical patterns and themes, through neglect of clear details
> of time and place, and the like, it is generally quickly recognizable
> by its composition. It runs far too smoothly.... Legend arranges its
> material in a simple and straightforward way; it detaches it from
> contemporary historical context, so that the latter will not confuse
> it; it knows only clearly outlined men who act from few and simple
> motives and the continuity of whose feelings and actions remains
> uninterrupted.[26]

It is this detachment from history, a typological structure, and a straight-
forwardness of narrative line which separate the poem and the homily from
Bede. The purpose of their narratives is to give voice to truths, and to the
institutionalization of those truths, be they the structures of the Mass or the
hierarchies of the Church. Political or historical accuracy here would only
muddle the directness of the Aelfrician parable. Put bluntly, Aelfric has no
interest in writing history.

But it is that very notion of "writing" which makes Auerbach's classi-
fication problematic here and which enables us to take his differentiation
between history and legend only so far. The works he addresses, Homer and
the Old Testament, appear to us in their received form as written texts, but
have their origins in oral recitation or in folk tradition. Their beginnings in
performance and in audience response, however, do not interest Auerbach.
While he acknowledges the issue, he concerns himself only with their status
as received documents of cultural styles (*Mimesis* 23). Now, in a sense, Aelfric stands in relation to his sources as Auerbach stands in relation to his
subjects: Bede and the kind of poetry exemplified by *Andreas* appear for
Aelfric as texts, rather than as traditions. They constitute the objects of
study, as well as the subjects of rescription. Aelfric's version of Imma rein-
vests, in a textual environment, in the legendary origins of stories which had
been historicized in their transmitted written form. In brief, Bede's story of
Imma begins as legend and becomes history; Aelfric takes that history and
transforms it into a legend for the literate life.

That transformation, as I have suggested, involves not simply rewriting
the tale but resituating it within a set of learned documents. More generally,
by grounding Imma's story in the reading of its records and the knowledge of
its analogues, Aelfric makes the understanding of the sacraments themselves
inseparable from the interpretation of texts. The power of the Mass is to be
felt here not only in its personal force or in its local, legendary aura but in its

situation in the dialogue of texts and readings which constitute the literate life. Reading Gregory augments the force of reading Bede, and central to this multiplication of *auctores* is the guiding sense of spiritual understanding as a form of interpretive canon formation. The syllabus of study constitutes itself as a repository of exempla and their explications. Aelfric leaves it to his readers to make those connections, to explore the relevance of Bede's narratives or Gregory's arguments to their own lives. In this, he vivifies his earlier affirmation of the two-fold need for *boclicum gewritum*: one to understand, the other to apply. That double charge informs the final moves of this brief homily. He asks the audience to read over *(oferrædan)* the stories of the Mass in Gregory, and in so doing, invites them to engage in that process of consideration and reflection which is the first aspect of full and spiritual literacy. By implication, the *weorc* which results from this process of reflection will be the proper performance of the sacrament: attendance at the Mass, recognition of its power, and its use in helping the souls of the living and dead. Literacy for Aelfric is thus a social practice as much as it is an intellectual skill. It defines the ways in which people engage with their peers, their lords, and their God. It offers a way of organizing groups into a readership for the authoritative documents of cultural and spiritual history.

Aelfric's conception of literate authority – and what one might call the homiletic persona which evolves from it – rests, I would argue, on the conscious appeals to such earlier *auctores* as Bede, Gregory, and elsewhere, Augustine. Their usefulness as models derives not solely from their own authority as fathers of the Church or scholars in themselves, but on their accomplishments as authors: on their production of a body of written texts whose knowledge as a whole is central to the understanding of their doctrine. For Bede and Augustine in particular, that body of texts finds itself catalogued in the booklists or retractions which close their major works and which survived to be transcribed and transmitted as a veritable biography of the intellectual life. They imply a notion of the canonicity of texts for reading and for teaching – an issue I will turn to presently – as well as the self-conscious creation of the self through the written oeuvre. It is this latter purpose, I suggest, which governs Aelfric's attentions to the collection and transcription of his works. He brings together the assembly of the Catholic Homilies into a unified whole, one which demands close reading as well as close writing. For what he stresses is the need for scribal accuracy in reproducing the integrity of his text.

> Nu bidde ic and halsige, on Godes naman, gif hwa ðas boc awritan wylle, þæt he hi geornlice gerihte be ðære bysne, þe-læs ðe we, þurh gymeleasum writerum, geleahtrode beon.

(I now pray and implore, in the name of God, if anyone will transcribe this book, that he carefully rectify it by the copy, lest, through negligent writers, we are blamed.) (2:2-3)

Aelfric offers here no casual assertion of his text's authority, but a carefully phrased, vernacular account of the technical terms of scriptorial production. The *bysne*, or copy, he refers to is the Latin *exemplum* from which the scribes would take their copy text. The verb Thorpe translates as "rectify," *gerihte*, is more literally, "to make right," and as such, translates precisely the Latin *corrigere*, to correct or align precisely on the page. That these injunctions form a part of Aelfric's larger conception of his textual enterprise is clear from their appearance in the preface to his *Grammar:* "Ic bidde nu on godes naman, gyf hwa ðas boc awritan wille, þæt he hi gerihte wel be ðære bysne."[27] My point in these examples is not to abstract a fully formed notion of textual criticism from Aelfric's remarks, nor is it to find in them the evidence for an Aelfrician scriptorial network. It is, instead, to call attention to the ways in which Aelfric defines his own authorial persona – that is, the ways in which he brings the reader's own attention to the texts and documents which both contribute towards and constitute his own, literary production. Aelfric is both reader and writer, and his injunctions to his audience fuse those activities as he directs them to be good readers of Bede and Gregory, while at the same time to be accurate rewriters of his own text.

The conception of a Christian literacy behind Aelfric's citations of patristic authors points to a canon of texts appropriate for spiritual education. But such a notion of a canon embraces more than a syllabus of study. It offers, as John Guillory has argued in another context, "a selection of values."[28] He continues: "Canonicity is not the property of the work itself but of its transmission, its relation to other works in a collocation of works." It is this systemic or relational conception of a canon which I think motivates the syncretism of eclectic source hunting of Aelfric. For by juxtaposing Bede and Gregory, Aelfric affirms the canonicity of both his sources in relation to each other; by calling attention to the need for scribal accuracy, he shows how the implied, canonical status of his own texts requires a fidelity in their transmission. In their shared company with source and in their pleas for textual integrity, Aelfric's works assert their own canonicity and, in effect, constitute a vernacular equivalent of the patristic, Latin sources which contribute to the canon for a spiritual readership.

To Bede, however, the question of the canon is less a matter of English and Latin, source and product, than it is a matter of the individual life and its place in a community of readers. The so-called "bibliography" which closes the *Ecclesiastical History* offers, at one level, the vision of a life defined by reading and writing. It complements our knowledge of the biographical details of Bede's life: his lack of worldly travel, his intense love of study, his commitment to the communities at Wearmouth and Jarrow, his fascination with the physicality of books themselves. But, at another level, the encyclopaedism of this appendix presents a program for a culture, and by implication, a reflection on the idea of canonicity itself. Coming, as it does, after the summary account of the work's chronological matter and after the brief autobiographical résumé, the bibliography presents a system of organization: a system whose constituent parts have meaning primarily in relation to each other and to the system as a whole. To follow Guillory, no single one of Bede's texts is "canonical" in itself; rather, it is the collocation of works and their participation in a structure of transmission which grant them a canonical status. It is, in these terms, not so much a "remarkable" individual achievement, as one recent critic has asserted (Fry, "Art of Bede"), as it is the product of and response to a community. Bede's oeuvre encompasses all the accepted forms of textual expression and offers commentaries on the canon of *auctores* for his readership. In so doing, it illustrates how canon formation is the activity both of selection and compilation, and it is this double agenda which informs his chronological summary as well. Here, in the précis of the *Ecclesiastical History* itself, Bede offers a selection culled not from the work of others but from himself. His order of dates, too, is itself a canon, a listing of the central events of world and English history each of which has meaning, like the texts which follow them, only in the system of the history they constitute.

In this closing synthesis of life and learning, events and texts, Bede reifies the nature of his own narrative authority. As he states in the brief autobiographical account which bridges the chronology and the bibliography, he has composed his history from sources "gleaned either from ancient documents, or from tradition, or from my own knowledge" ("prout uel ex litteris antiquorum uel ex traditione maiorum uel ex mea ipse cognitione scire potui," 5.24; *EH* 566-7). Texts, tradition, and experience stand side-by-side in the work's final chapter, and in the end, the *Ecclesiastical History* seems to enjoin its reader to find himself in the communities which both give shape to and are formed by Bede's achievement. The reader is invited to resituate himself as Bede as done: to find a place in the history of England, the experiences of life, and the syllabus of study.

The act of reading, then, for Bede as well as Aelfric becomes a way of aligning the individual within a social framework. Both writers illustrate the confrontation of a Christian and an alien literacy, and both posit a new textual ideal. For Bede, it is the written Latin *historia* ranged against the orally transmitted *fabula* of the releasing letters. For Aelfric it is the newly Englished Gregory, offered now to be read in tandem with his own vernacular version of a Bedean legend. Sorcery and runology meet their defeat or their denial as new texts replace them. The religious rites of the Mass or the vernacular translations of spiritual classics become the new, reordering performances of Christian society. Literacy and textuality – as themes, as problems, or as polemics – move beyond the purely historical question of learning to read. They come to signify a way of organizing the canonical documents of culture, a way of grounding anew the public education in the signs of life. For Imma and his readers, such signs are to be found in the symbolically charged power of the Mass. For Bede and his rewriters, that power is inseparable from the textually informed understanding of the sacraments. In the end, it is not the mere letter which releases. *Drycræft* and a faith in runes pose a challenge to the conventions of interpretation which give shape to culture and which grant belief in the miracles of God and his sacraments. The central purpose of conversion becomes the reorientation of a culture and its members away from a reliance on the lore of mystical characters and towards an understanding of the symbolism inherent in religious rites. Such a conversion necessitates, in turn, a new canon of texts to guide the Christian in the recognition of those symbols. Such texts will appear not in the runic shapes of old epigraphy, but in the alphabet of the new learning, and it is this Roman alphabet, as well as the Roman Church, which Bede and his inheritors celebrate, as the conversion of the English people becomes a conversion to a way of being as well as to a way of reading.

Notes

1. For critical analyses of the story of Imma, see R. I. Page, "Anglo-Saxon Runes and Magic," *Journal of the British Archaeological Association* 27 (1964): 14-31; Joel T. Rosenthal, "Bede's Use of Miracles in 'The Ecclesiastical History'," *Traditio* 31 (1975): 328-35; Calvin Kendall, "Bede's *Historia Ecclesiastica*: The Rhetoric of Faith," in J. J. Murphy, ed., *Medieval Eloquence* (Berkeley and Los Angeles, 1978), 145-72. Throughout this paper, all quotations and translations from Bede's Latin will be from Bertram Colgrave and R. A. B. Mynors, eds., *Bede's Ecclesiastical History of the English People* (Oxford, 1969), and cited in the text as *EH*. All quotations and translations from the Old English version of the History will be from Thomas Miller, ed., *The Old English Version of Bede's Ecclesiastical History of the English People,* Early English Text Society, Original Series 95,96 (London, 1890-91).

2. "Hortatorius Sermo De Efficacia Sanctae Missae," in Benjamin Thorpe, ed., *Aelfric Sermones Catholici,* 2 vols. (London, 1844-46), 2:356-59.

3. On the grammar of the passage and a review of earlier scholarship on its translation into both Old and Modern English, see Page, "Anglo-Saxon Runes and Magic," 21-24.

4. E. G. Stanley, *The Search for Anglo-Saxon Paganism* (Cambridge, 1975). For evidence and arguments against the magical uses of runology in England, see Page, "Anglo-Saxon Runes and Magic," and his later reformulations in *An Introduction to English Runes* (London, 1973), 105-8.

5. For an approach to symbolism in medieval Christian rite and ritual, with particular reference to debates on the Eucharist, see Brian Stock, *The Implications of Literacy* (Princeton, 1983), 241-59, especially the following remarks on the Augustinian conception of the sign and act in the performance of the sacrament: "... the sacraments were viewed as symbolic actions in which interpretation formed an integral part of enactment" (258). It lies in this inherently symbolic nature of the sacrament, and the necessity of its interpretation, that I see the function of the Mass in the story of Imma and the implicit tensions between oral and written, sign and symbol in the *History* as a whole.

6. See Rosenthal and the earlier studies cited therein. More recent assessments include those of J. N. Stephens, "Bede's Ecclesiastical History," *History,* n.s. 62 (1977): 1-14; Benedicta Ward, *Miracles and the Medieval Mind* (Philadelphia, 1982); and her earlier article, "Miracles and History: A Reconsideration of the Miracle Stories Used by Bede," in Gerald Bonner, ed., *Famulus Christi* (London, 1976), 70-76.

7. See the approaches enshrined in Dorothy Whitelock's edition of *Sweet's Anglo-Saxon Reader,* 15th ed. (Oxford, 1967), in Frederic G. Cassidy and Richard N. Ringler, *Bright's Old English Grammar and Reader,* 3rd ed. (New York, 1971), and in C. L. Wrenn, *A Study of Old English Literature* (London, 1967). For a succinct review of standard interpretive problems, with a full bibliography and critical apparatus, see Stanley Greenfield and Daniel G. Calder, *A New Critical History of Old English Literature* (New York, 1985), 227-31.

8. On the need to posit an "oral" origin for archaic literatures, see the remarks in Charles Segal, "Greek Tragedy: Writing, Truth, and the Representation of the Self," in his *Interpreting Greek Tragedy: Myth, Poetry, Text* (Ithaca, 1986), 75-109. Segal announces that the "search for the preliterate substratum [in Greek literature] may be another form of western man's perpetual longing for a primordial world of innocence and simplicity" and of "print culture's nostalgia for oral culture" (108).

9. I quote from the edition and translation in Susan D. Fuller, "Pagan Charms in Tenth-Century Saxony? The Function of the Meresburg Charms," *Monatsheft* 72 (1980): 162-70.

10. In her translation of the charm, Fuller assumes that the *idisi* are "valkyries," although without explanation. For Tacitus on prophetic women, see *Germania* 8, quoted in Audrey L. Meaney, "The *Ides* of the Cotton Gnomic Poem," *Medium Aevum* 48 (1979): 23-39.

11. See Georges Dumézil, *Gods of the Ancient Northmen,* ed. and trans. Einar Haugen, et al. (Berkeley and Los Angeles, 1984), 40, citing material from the old Norse *Grimnismál* 36; and Helen Damico, *Beowulf's Wealhtheow and the Valkyrie Tradition* (Madison, 1984), 43-44. For the *Brot* see Dumézil, 40, who quotes, "enn þu, gramr, ridir, glaums andvani, / fiotri fatladr i fianda lið," and explains: "He is fettered by the *herfjotur,* 'army fetter,' the enchantment that paralyzes the warrior."

12. "Allar þessar íþróttir kenndi hann með runum ok ljoðum þeim, er galdrar heita." *Ynglingasaga* ch.7, in Snorri Sturluson, *Heimskringla I,* ed. Bjarni Aðalbjarnarson, Islensk Fornrit 26 (Reykjavik, 1941), 19.

13. Two studies which assess these problems directly, in Aelfric's England and Snorri's Iceland, are Karen Louise Jolly, "Anglo-Saxon Charms in the Context of a Christian World View," *Journal of Medieval History* 11 (1985): 279-93, and Arthur D. Mosher, "The Story of Baldr's Death: The Inadequacy of Myth in the Light of Christian Faith," *Scandinavian Studies* 55 (1983): 305-15.

14. See Dumézil, 40; Mosher; and Roberta Frank, "Snorri and the Mead of Poetry," in Ursula Dronke, et al., eds., *Speculum Norroennum: Norse Studies in Memory of Gabriel Turville-Petre* (Odense, 1981), 155-70.

15. Irenaeus of Lyon, *Contra Haereseos,* quoted and discussed in Thomas N. Rendall, "Bondage and Freeing from Bondage in Old English Religious Poetry," *Journal of English and Germanic Philology* 73 (1974): 497-512, who also traces the influence of this particular formulation on Origen, Augustine, and Gregory, and on the poetry of Cynewulf and *Andreas.*

16. On the typologies of what he labels "hagiographic romance" (i.e., with the governing pattern of exile, capture, torture, release, and homecoming) with special reference to Old English narrative, see Alvin A. Lee, *The Guest-Hall of Eden* (New Haven, 1971). For a more specialized study, bearing directly on my reading of *Andreas* in this paper, see James W. Earl, "The Typological Structure of *Andreas*," in John D. Niles, ed., *Old English Literature in Context* (Totowa, NJ, 1980), 66-89.

17. On some contemporary conceptions of *fabulae* and their place in public life, see Patrick Wormald, "Bede, *Beowulf,* and the Conversion of the Anglo-Saxon Aristocracy," in Robert T. Farrell, ed., *Bede and Anglo-Saxon England,* British Archaeological Reports 46 (Oxford, 1978), 32-85, especially 42-4. In particular, Wormald calls attention to the uses of *fabula* in Alcuin and in ecclesiastical writings to refer to pagan or secular literature (either classical or Germanic), in contrast to Christian scripture or hagiography. Wormald assumes that in the story of Imma, Bede himself "had used the word *fabulae* of stories about runes" (44), although there are no runes explicitly mentioned in Bede's Latin; and it seems clear at this point (*contra* Wormald) that Bede's mention of *fabulae* is directed to a different literary purpose than his mere condemnation of the *libri gentilium fabulae saeculares* in his commentary on Samuel (44 and 78 n.57).

18. "... uetere usus augurio, ne superuentu suo, siquid maleficae artis habuissent, eum superando deciperent" (*EH* 74-5).

19. "At illi non daemonica sed diuina uirtute praediti ueniebant, crucem pro uexillo ferentes argenteam, et imaginem Domini Saluatoris in tabula depictam.... " (*EH* 74-5).

20. On Germanic *faihian as the general verb for the act of runic epigraphy (signalling coloring as well as writing), and its traditional pairing with *writan in early inscriptions, see Lucien Musset, *Introduction à la Runologie* (Paris, 1965), 89-90; Richard L. Morris, "Northwest-Germanic *Run* - 'Rune': A Case of Homonymy with Go. *runa*, 'mystery'," *Beiträge zur Geschichte der deutschen Sprache und Literatur* 107 (1985): 344-58.

21. See the bibliography assembled in Jan de Vries, *Altgermanische Religionsgeschichte*, 2 vols. (Berlin, 1935-37), ix-xlix, citing the studies of Simrock, Heinzel, and Mögk; and the summary account in Dumézil, 21-5. For more recent reassessments of the notion of a "liquid poetics" in Indo-European cultures, see Frank; the study of Bruce Lincoln, *Myth, Cosmos, and Society: Indo-European Themes of Creation and Destruction* (Cambridge, MA, 1986), 65-86, 196-7, and the bibliography cited throughout his discussion. In the following account I rely on the materials collected in Wendy Doniger O'Flaherty, trans., *The Rig-Veda* (Baltimore, 1981) for Sanskrit materials and in Kuno Meyer, "The Boyhood Exploits of Finn," *Eiru* 1 (1903):186-89, for Old Irish traditions.

22. *Enarratio in Psalmos* 46.1, in *Corpus Christianorum, Series Latina*, 38.529, cited and translated in André Crépin, "Bede and the Vernacular," in *Famulus Christi*, 172. For a survey of commentary on the passages in Leviticus 11.3 and Deuteronomy 14.6 which articulate the ideals of *ruminatio*, see Crépin's extended n.6, 187-89.

23. For other approaches to Caedmon in the heritage of monastic learning, see Donald W. Fritz, "Caedmon: A Monastic Exegete," *American Benedictine Review* 25 (1974): 351-63, and more generally, Donald K. Fry, "The Art of Bede, II: The Reliable Narrator as Persona," *Acta* 6 (1982): 63-82.

24. For a discussion of this imagery, see Simon Keynes, *The Diplomas of King Aethelred 'The Unready' 978-1016* (Cambridge, 1980), 136-38, working from the text of Aelfric's *De Populo Israhel*, in J. C. Pope, ed., *Homilies of Aelfric*, Early English Text Society, Original Series 260 (London, 1968), 259.

25. All quotations from *Andreas* are from Kenneth R. Brooks, ed., *Andreas and the Fates of the Apostles* (Oxford, 1961).

26. Erich Auerbach, *Mimesis*, trans. Willard R. Trask (Princeton, 1953), 19.

27. Julius Zupitza, ed., *Aelfrics Grammatik und Glossar* (Berlin, 1880), 3.

28. John Guillory, "Canonical and Non-Canonical: A Critique of the Current Debate," *ELH: A Journal of English Literary History* 54 (1987):483-527. This and the following quotation are from 488 and 494, respectively.

FROM BRIGANDAGE TO JUSTICE

CHARLEMAGNE, 785-794

THOMAS F. X. NOBLE

One of the more memorable passages in Einhard's life of Charlemagne comes in Chapter 24 when the author tells us that "He took great pleasure in the books of Saint Augustine and especially in those which are called 'The City of God'."[1] I have often wondered how we are to understand this apparently simple and straightforward statement. Augustine's magisterial treatise is one of the most difficult, not to mention longest, books ever written and Charlemagne, although an undoubted enthusiast, was no intellectual. I am pretty certain, though, that however Charlemagne got his acquaintance with "The City of God," he will have been struck by the passage in Book 4 chapter 4, where Augustine wrote:

> Remove justice, and what are kingdoms but gangs of criminals on a large scale? What are criminal gangs but petty kingdoms? A gang is a group of men under the command of a leader, bound by a compact of association, in which plunder is divided according to an agreed convention.

> If this villainy wins so many recruits from the ranks of the demoralized that it acquires territory, establishes a base, captures cities and subdues peoples, it then openly arrogates to itself the title of kingdom, which is conferred on it in the eyes of the world, not by the renunciation of aggression but by the attainment of impunity.[2]

Charlemagne was manifestly aggressive and he was, and was acknowledged to be, a great conqueror. As Tim Reuter has recently reminded us, Charlemagne was also an accomplished plunderer.[3] He seems almost ideally suited to be labeled a gang leader, a criminal, a brigand, in Augustine's sense. But Charlemagne was also powerfully interested in justice, and so it may have been that Augustine's words showed him how he might remove from himself the charge of criminality.

Justice, along with humility, peace, wisdom, clemency and other Christian values, was at the center of Charlemagne's ethos of rulership. This is reasonably well known and widely acknowledged.[4] In this essay, however, I wish to draw attention to the time when that ethos took shape, and to the enactments by means of which it was implemented in a public way for the kingdom of the Franks. Specifically, then, I shall be focusing on the years from about 785 to 794, and on the loyalty oaths of 789 and 792/93, on the *Admonitio Generalis* of 789, on the *Libri Carolini* of 790-93, and briefly on the canons of the Council of Frankfurt of 794. My reasons for concentrating on those particular years, and on those specific enactments, will be explained in due course, but my subsequent interpretations will be a bit clearer if I establish a few preliminary points.

Perhaps chief among these preliminaries is the need to decide when and how Carolus became *Magnus*. The issue might seem so obvious, or unimportant, as to need no emphasis, but I think that it has, in fact, been overlooked. We do very little "great man" history these days, and our studies are probably all the better for that – though princes in the kingdom of *Annales* (Georges Duby and Jacques Le Goff) recently announced that we could do biography again, so "great men," including, one hopes, females, may make a comeback. But an intellectually toxic waste from the great man days makes it too easy to suppose that great men were always great, that they did not show development, change, hesitation, even failure. F. L. Ganshof once told me of meeting a very excited Joseph Calmette at a conference in Paris and of being upbraided by him for publishing an article later translated into English as "Charlemagne's Failure," because, Calmette insisted, Charlemagne was a great man and great men just do not have failures.[5] I happen to think that Charles deserves his adjective, and I am going to discuss when and why he earned it. In doing so I will have the company of a good many of Charles's contemporaries. If one were to leave out official *intitulationes,* the kinds of titles that issued from the royal chancery, and that appeared in diplomas, capitularies and letters, one would find that the tendency to describe Charles in increasingly grander terms began in the mid-780s, and then continued throughout the reign. In other words, I shall draw attention to the very period when Charlemagne seems to have inspired the adulation, to have unlocked the muses, of his contemporaries.

Now, as I am more interested in Charles himself than I am in his contemporaries, one may well ask if there is any warrant to attempt to discover Charles's ethos of rulership in a series of public acts and state papers. This is an old problem, by no means confined to the reign of Charlemagne, and many historians have addressed it in one way or another. It has often been lamented that while we know more about Charlemagne than about any ruler before or after him for some centuries in each direction, we mostly know what he did and not what he believed or thought. Ganshof, on the contrary, did think it possible to identify what he called Charlemagne's "ruler personality" in his public acts and actions, but formidable authorities such as Donald Bullough have doubted that, in the almost total absence of letters, diaries or other personal and intimate records, we can really know much about Charlemagne's personality.[6] I agree with Bullough, but I do not think he was answering Ganshof head on. That is, I think it is extremely difficult, perhaps indeed impossible, to ascertain what kind of a human being Charlemagne was, but I do think that his ideas and ideology, his fundamental plans and goals as a ruler, are recoverable from the surviving record. And it was those ideas and plans that Ganshof had in mind.

Recent studies suggest that my efforts may be complicated, perhaps contradicted, by the considerable continuity that is evident between Charlemagne's reign and that of his father, Pepin III. Scholars, Pierre Riché and Jean Hubert chief among them, have been pointing to the reign of Pepin as the true beginning of the "Carolingian Renaissance," but I think that their zeal has been excessive.[7] Church reform did, it is true, begin in the time of Boniface, and it was continued in Pepin's age through the efforts of Chrodegang and Fulrad, but it was in Charlemagne's time that the resources of the Carolingian state were enthusiastically committed with results unimaginable in the previous reign. The first stirrings of Carolingian architecture may be discernible at St. Denis or Lorsch, but these humble beginnings compare unfavorably with the spectacular projects initiated in the late 780s. The enigmatic Gundohinus Gospels are surely no precedent for the magnificent books produced at Charlemagne's court. Pepin brought chant masters from Rome, while Charlemagne Romanized much of the liturgy and liturgified his state. Education was given a prominence in Charlemagne's time unmatched in all previous Frankish experience. Pepin's court, about which we know almost nothing, was never the nerve center and command control that Charlemagne's court was. But the greatest difference of all is that in Pepin's time reform extended only to the Church, whereas in Charles' era Church and kingdom were identified with one another and reformed simultaneously. I do not mean to suggest that Charlemagne broke with his father, nor even that their goals and aspirations were essentially different. It is the scale of activities in the two reigns that is dramatically dissimilar. Change might be too strong a word but continuity is no less misleading except, ironically, in military affairs. Indeed, I have argued elsewhere that in military affairs Charlemagne was very much the heir of his father and grandfather.[8] Thus, without wishing to seem contrary, I am denying continuity where many scholars now detect it, and positing continuity where most scholars have always denied it.

One final preliminary point may be made, and it is in a way the essence and summation of all the others. By drawing attention to one specific period within Charlemagne's reign, indeed by suggesting that the period from about 785 to 794 is a discrete period, I am implying that the reign was perhaps made up of several periods. It is a reasonable supposition that the one fact, or date, from Charlemagne's reign that is known to the proverbial schoolboy is the imperial coronation of 800, the event that prompted Viscount Bryce to say that had it not happened the history of the world would have been different.[9] I don't know if that is true, but I am pretty sure that the histories of Charlemagne's reign would have been different without the coronation. At the least, there would not have been so vividly in evidence a tendency to interpret everything before 800 as somehow a prelude to the coronation. Events and developments from the period between 768 and 800 might have been allowed to gain or to lose their own significance in their own time and context. I am going to suggest later that the coronation was an anticlimax to the very developments that will be at the center of our concerns, but I will assert now that it has long exerted a distorting force in the historiography of the reign.

No less distorting has been the approach most evident in the classic treatments of Mühlbacher, Kleinclausz and Halphen.[10] Their works broke the reign down into topics, usually military, administrative-governmental, and intellectual, and in so doing destroyed all hope of seeing simultaneity, contingency, change, continuity and design. The great break with this customary approach was made by Ganshof, who year after year devoted his seminar in Ghent to the close study of Charlemagne's reign on a year-by-year basis. He never wrote the great book on Charlemagne that he promised in the thirties, but in an article which he published in *Speculum* in 1949 he showed what that book would have been like.[11] That article, and many related studies, have been in my mind since Richard Sullivan introduced me to Carolingian history in 1970, and they deeply influenced the way I studied Charlemagne's Italian policy in the 770s and 780s in the relevant sections of *The Republic of St. Peter*.[12] Basically, Ganshof argued for a chronological approach that identified, and that sought to understand on their own terms, the major periods of Charlemagne's reign. These were: First, an exceedingly inauspicious beginning between 768 and 771 when Charles shared rule with his brother Carlomann; second, an ambitious, energetic but largely aimless stretch in the 770s that culminated in a series of disasters in 778 and 779; third, a cautious new beginning in about 781; fourth, a period of confidence and achievement, briefly interrupted in 791-92, running from about 789 to the issuance of the "Programmatic Capitulary" of 802; fifth, a period of imperial consolidation running down to about 810; and, sixth, a few final years of decline as a sick old man faced new challenges without the energy of his youth or the companions of his lifetime. It is, then, on the fourth of Ganshof's periods that I wish to focus, but I aim to take it back a little before 789, and to stop short of the coronation or of the famous capitularies of 802.

Even if Ganshof's overall chronological, or perhaps periodic, approach has not been as widely adopted as it deserves, it is true that the 780s have been recognized as an important period in the reign. In fresh and crucial studies Donald Bullough has emphasized that it was only in this decade, and above all after 782 when Alcuin came to court, that Charlemagne had assembled the personnel who would help formulate and implement the great policy initiatives of the reign.[13] The first great Carolingian book, the Godescalc Evangelistary, was produced between 781 and 783 and inaugurated the stunning series of books from Charlemagne's reign.[14] The earliest work on the Aachen complex of buildings must date from about 788 and the beginnings of St. Riquier and the rebuilding of the cathedral of Metz and the abbatial of Fulda fall in these same years.[15] In about 786 Charlemagne received from Rome a great Mass book which his palace scholars, chiefly Benedict of Aniane, set to work revising.[16] In 786 Paul the Deacon's new lectionary was issued for churches in the Frankish realm.[17] In 787 Charlemagne sent to Rome for an authentic copy of the Rule of St. Benedict, the better to promote monastic order in his kingdom.[18] In 789 a large part of the *Dionysio-Hadriana,* a collection of canon law received at court in 774 or shortly thereafter, was promulgated.[19] These years saw coinage reforms and adjustments in the standards for weights and measures.[20] The institution of the *missi dominici* was regularized for the whole kingdom between 779 and 789.[21] The years 781 and 787 saw comprehensive territorial settlements in Italy.[22] Examples could be multiplied considerably, but I think it will be clear that the middle to late 780s represented for Charlemagne and his associates a period of heavy activity on a variety of fronts. Was this mere coincidence, or is it evidence of intention, of design? And if all of this activity was planned, was there any coherent notion behind the plan? Let us turn now to my three case studies to see if we can answer these questions.

First, then, the loyalty oaths. In 789, and then again in 792, Charlemagne sent special *missi* throughout his realm to receive, presumably from all free men, an oath of loyalty that was to be sworn in the following words: "I so and so promise to my lord King Charles and to his sons that I am faithful and that I will be so all the days of my life without fraud or evil intention."[23]

The words of the oath survive in one legation's edict and we have another *breviarium* from Aquitaine which indicates that the oath was also sworn there.[24] It appears that the oath was required throughout the realm and not just in the heartlands, or in recently conquered areas, or from Frankish nobles. In 792 another effort was made to get the oath sworn by those who had been missed in 789, because some men had raised the standard of rebellion against Charles, and had plotted against his life, advancing as their defense that they had not sworn fidelity to the king and therefore had done him no wrong.[25]

The surviving texts say that the oath was an *antiqua consuetudo* but legal historians agree that by Charlemagne's time the practice was more ancient than customary.[26] What prompted Charles to institute, or to revive, the oath at this juncture? It has often been suggested that the original oath, the one of 789, can be tied to the rebellion in Thuringia in 785 or 786 of a local notable named Hardrad. This is possible, but I wonder why Charles waited so long – three or four years – to demand the oaths, and why this rebellion, just one among many as Karl Brunner has reminded us, evoked such a novel response.

To me it is interesting to note that the oaths were first required in 789 and that they had the effect of treating all free men in the kingdom in just the same way. In fact, I see a convergence of possibilities that helps to explain the meaning of these oaths. Thuringia had caused problems for the rulers of the Franks since the sixth century, but after Hardrad's misadventures no more trouble arose in this quarter. In the years between 782 and 785 Charles issued his first Saxon capitulary.[27] He was to be sorely deceived, but at that time he believed that he had put an end to the Franks' long standing problems with their neighbors to the northeast. In 781 Charles had introduced his sons Pepin and Louis into Italy and Aquitaine as kings.[28] Independent kingships were a concession to these regions, but royal lines confined inside the Carolingian family significantly mitigated that concession and loudly broadcast the message of the essential unity of the kingdom as a whole.[29] The 780s saw two major territorial settlements in Italy that had the net result of defining the possessions of the Franks, the popes, the Byzantines and the Lombards of Benevento.[30] In 786 Charles thought that he had reduced Brittany to subjection, although, as we know, he was no more successful than any subsequent French government in that effort.[31] In 788 Tassilo of Bavaria was removed from power, and the independent Bavarian ducal line was eliminated.[32] In 787 Duke Arichis of Benevento was brought to heel. He had royal Lombard blood in his veins, was related to the troublesome Bavarian duke, and had set himself up as the focus of anti-Carolingian sentiment in Italy. He represented a very real threat to Charlemagne.[33]

Looking at these developments from another angle permits us to see that the loyalty oaths did not follow exclusively upon the revolt of Hardrad, but that they followed a long period of geo-political consolidation. I am not sure that I agree with Karl Brunner that Charles created by these oaths an *Untertanenverband* because I suspect that *Untertanen*, subjects, is anachronistic, but I most heartily agree that a *Verband,* a union or association, was created. What did it replace? Basically the *regnum Francorum* had been since Clovis's time a confederation of *regna* bound together by different kinds of alliances with the *rex Francorum.* Scholars such as Walter Kienast, Walter Schlesinger and Karl-Ferdinand Werner have repeatedly emphasized that these *regna* – not all of which were ever kingdoms in the strict sense – were the real building blocks, not only of the Frankish realm, but in reality of continental Europe.[34] In other words, Charlemagne's military, diplomatic and political initiatives were capped by the loyalty oaths that all free man had to swear to him and to his royal Frankish sons.

It stretches credulity to see it as a coincidence that in about 794 Paulinus of Aquileia referred to Charles as "gubernator omnium Christianorum," and that official texts from 789 refer to the *populus Christianus,* or to the *populus Dei,* over whom Charles ruled.[35] By 794 Alcuin, perhaps Charlemagne's closest adviser, had begun regularly to refer to the people in the *regnum Francorum* as the *populus Christianus.*[36] The oaths gave institutional expression to, and provided a legal mechanism for perpetuating, a new kind of regime. It was in a way a Pauline community, where ethnic differences were unimportant, or an Augustinian *Civitas Dei,* in which only a shared faith in Christ mattered. It had not many peoples but one, and these peoples had one *rex,* who was not their conqueror or their ally, but rather their *gubernator,* their helmsman. Where that helmsman was steering was made clear in another of 789's major actions, the *Admonitio Generalis.*

If a person were to ask me what one document he or she might read to form an impression of Charlemagne's program of royal government, I would without hesitation recommend the great capitulary of 789 called the *Admonitio Generalis,* and all the more so now that it is available in a complete English translation by David King.[37] Three of Charlemagne's capitularies are almost equal in length, and significantly longer than all the others: The *Capitulare de villis,* the so-called Programmatic Capitulary of 802, and the *Admonitio.* The *Capitulare de villis* is a text of great importance to the student of Carolingian institutional and economic history, but it falls outside our present field of vision. The Programmatic Capitulary and the *Admonitio* are remarkably similar, and if it would not take me too far afield I think I could demonstrate satisfactorily that the former is really only a repetition of the latter with some slight adjustments in emphasis. Recently a new capitulary has been discovered from the years just after the Programmatic Capitulary and its concerns are almost exactly those of its two well-known predecessors.[38] The *Admonitio,* then, is the great capitulary of the reign. This is evident enough on the plain testimony of the text itself, to which we shall turn in a moment, but it also emerges from a comparison of this capitulary with those that preceded it in Charles's reign. There are several of these and they are marked, in my view, by two characteristics: They are unsystematic and ad hoc. That is, they contain rather jumbled sets of provisions dealing in quite specific ways with particular problems. In 789, with the *Admonitio,* a completely different spirit is in the air. This text is more consistent, more general, and more manifestly programmatic.[39]

In order to come to terms with the place of the *Admonitio* in Charlemagne's reign, we need to reflect for a moment on capitularies in general. Recent work has brought considerable refinement to our understanding of the preparation and purpose of these immensely significant documents. They are neither legal nor legislative texts in the strict sense of the terms. They are more like executive orders, but they were fully binding upon all persons or institutions specified in their provisions. Their force derived from the royal *bannum,* the royal right to command. But they were not exclusively royal enactments. Ganshof, in his still indispensable study of the capitularies, overemphasized the royal and oral nature of the documents.[40] He asserted that they flowed solely from royal authority and that they were promulgated orally with the written texts being at best of secondary significance and possibly irrelevant. Today, Ganshof's views have been modified in three respects. First, the capitularies are viewed as the product of deliberations that probably took place on two sequential levels. At the palace the king and his closest advisers prepared what we might think of as an agenda, and then at a *placitum generale,* at a public assembly of the Franks, the king undertook wide-ranging consultations that resulted in the oral and public promulgation of the actual capitulary. This process is neatly characterized in Hincmar's treatise *De ordine palatii* that comes from the late ninth century but that repeats significant parts of a much earlier treatise by Adalhard.[41] It is no wonder that scholars such as Jürgen Hannig, Janet Nelson and Gerhard Schmitz have begun speaking of consensus politics in the Carolingian world.[42] Second, it is now argued that it was the *missi* traversing the realm, and not the words of the king at the assembly, that played the decisive role in promulgating capitularies. The royal will is increasingly seen as constituent, rather than as exclusive. Finally, more attention is now being paid to the significance of the written text, as opposed to the oral order. The implications here are very important for our understanding of the degree of depersonalization and bureaucratization of Carolingian government, and this is currently the most active area of research in capitulary studies. Scholars are studying the transmission of particular texts, the compilation of collections of capitularies, and the whole problem of dissemination in an effort to better understand these critically significant texts.

Let me reformulate these remarks about capitularies with specific reference to the circumstances surrounding the *Admonitio*. I noted earlier that prominent among the reforms of the 780s was the one that streamlined and regularized the institution of the *missi dominici*. Can it be a mere coincidence that immediately after that reform Charlemagne issued the requirement for the loyalty oaths – oaths that had to be sworn before the *missi* – and then published the first great programmatic capitulary of the reign? I think that this is no coincidence at all and it squares with everything else that I have been able to learn about Charlemagne. It was his custom to study matters closely, get the appropriate mechanisms into place, and then to act. After the 770s there was very little wasted motion in this reign and there was never, as far as I can see, any gratuitous ideological posturing. It is also worth noting that the text of the *Admonitio* says explicitly, in its first lines, that it was the product of deliberations between Charlemagne and his priests and counsellors.[43] Following this lead, I can relate my remarks back to an earlier observation about the late 780s as the time when Charlemagne finally had his team together. In this connection it is especially important that the spirit of Alcuin broods over the *Admonitio*; that is, with Bullough, I agree with Schiebe that Alcuin is the virtual author of the text.[44] I shall return to the implications of this fact. For now I wish only to call attention to the context of the *Admonitio* in court and consultation. And, I ought to add, I do not think that this somehow reduces the significance of Charlemagne's role in the formulation of his own edicts. I think that it actually permits us to see how those edicts were formulated. Finally, it must be significant that the *Admonitio* is one of the most widely disseminated of all Carolingian capitularies.

What exactly did Charlemagne say now that he and his advisers had found their voice and had put in place the network to broadcast it? In external form the *Admonitio* is peculiar in several respects. It begins with the longest prologue of any capitulary from the whole Carolingian period. The prologue is followed by fifty-nine canons adopted from the *Dionysio-Hadriana* canonical collection given to Charlemagne by Hadrian I in about 774.[45] In 747 Pepin III promulgated some canonical material from the Dionysian collection that he had been sent by Pope Zachary,[46] so the 789 canons represent a second Frankish attempt to impose a substantial body of what then passed for Roman canon law. The sixtieth *capitulum* is, in a way, another introduction, this time summing up the Dionysian material and pointing to the twenty-one original *capitula* with which the text continues. The document ends with the longest epilogue of any capitulary.

The prologue sets the tone for the whole. Charlemagne compares himself to Josiah in "visitation, correction and admonition." Charles stresses that he has to set a good example, and that the bishops of the realm also have to be mindful of the example they set for those entrusted to their care. Interestingly, Charles states that he and the bishops have to seize the example provided by the ancient councils and canons.

Once into the text, the priority of faith becomes apparent. *Capitulum* 1, from the *Dionysio-Hadriana*, forbids association with excommunicated persons, and *capitulum* 61, the first substantive one in the purely Frankish part of the collection, demands that the holy catholic faith be taught. The text concludes with a profession of faith, that is an elementary commentary on the Nicene creed.

Again and again the text returns to the idea of teaching and preaching. Schools must be established, teachers appointed, books collected, corrected and copied. Bishops must preach, and must see to it that their subordinate clergy preach too. But all preachers must adhere to the canonical books and to the catholic fathers. No one is free to innovate. Nothing less than salvation is at stake. It is interesting to note that passages from the *Admonitio* are taken over verbatim in the famous *Epistola de litteris colendis*.[47] That document, a letter to Abbot Baugolf of Fulda commanding that a school be established according to certain prescribed guidelines, taken by itself, simply cannot present Charlemagne's interest in education in the kind of grand and programmatic context that is offered by the same provisions when they appear as part of the *Admonitio*. Charlemagne's interest in education began early in his reign and was a constant concern throughout. It was not until 789, however, that educational methods and fundamental goals were brought into close juxtaposition in one program.[48]

The *Admonitio* promotes salvation in two other ways besides education. First, it virtually incorporates the decalogue as a component of the public law of the realm.[49] It does this explicitly and makes its supervision a key responsibility of both the secular and the ecclesiastical ruling apparatus. Second, the *capitula* provide a whole series of negative and positive guidelines for public and private conduct. People are enjoined to seek peace, concord, and justice, for example. Honest weights and measures are to be used. Hostels are to be established for the poor, for pilgrims and for travelers. Perjury, indeed falsehood of every sort, is to be avoided as are avarice, malice, swindling and vagrancy. In short, sins are identified for avoidance and good works are specified for performance.

The symphonic elegance of the *Admonitio* is clearest of all in the way in which the epilogue re-sounds, in order, each of the major themes of the body of the work. Faith comes first, and thus we have a short credal statement. Then sins are to be avoided, and a long list of them is set down. Finally, Christian virtues are to be cultivated and good works accomplished. As expected, lists of both are provided. Josef Fleckenstein has succinctly characterized the *Admonitio* as a requirement "errata corrigere, superflua abscindere, recta cohartare."[50] It would be hard to improve on that.

Much of what the *Admonitio* means is explicit in what it says, but there are a few things that are implicit in both the text and its context. Let us note a few of these implicit points and then draw some general conclusions. Among many possibilities, three seem particularly important to me.

First, it is striking that just as Charles set himself up as an example and as a teacher, comparable images and expressions appeared elsewhere in the sources. Paul the Deacon, Alcuin and Angilbert, for example, borrowed the *rex doctus* image from Venantius Fortunatus and applied it to Charles.[51] Theodulf and Alcuin also spoke of Charles as *doctor, praedicator* and *rector,* and these themes were also sounded in the dedicatory verses to the Godescalc Evangelistary, produced in Charlemagne's court circle.[52] Peter Godman has shown that the force of these expressions was to emphasize the profound responsibility felt by Charles and those closest to him for the right teaching, the right leading, of those under their care. Charles was not *rex doctus* as a learned man and as the promoter of letters and the founder of a Renaissance. He was instead holder of a charge to preach and to teach like that of a bishop.[53]

Second, it is surely no accident that in these middle years of Charles's reign both official texts – the *Admonitio* for example – and private writings began to refer to kingship not as an *officium* but as a *ministerium.* The actual word *ministerium* does not become common until the reign of Louis the Pious, but the ideas which it represented had already begun emerging in the time of Pepin, and assumed clarity and coherence in the 780s and 790s. Kingship involved, in this ministerial conception, less the privilege of command than the burden of service. Charles would be judged according to whether he had led his people to salvation or to perdition. His leadership was inherent in the personal example he set for those around him.[54] The ideal here is undoubtedly Gregorian, and it stems, at least ultimately it does, from the *Pastoral Rule,* the great book in which Gregory set forth his ideas about the life of service that was entailed in the office of a bishop. For years scholars have, quite properly, devoted much attention to exploring classical, scriptural and Augustinian influences on Carolingian political thought. The impact of Gregory the Great has usually only been acknowledged in passing, if at all.[55] It deserves a full-scale study, both for its own sake and because of Gregory's acknowledged influence upon the Anglo-Saxons, a number of whom, beginning with Boniface, had direct access to and influence upon the evolving Carolingian regime. The royal ideal in the *Admonitio,* and in many contemporary sources, sounds, to mention but one example of this possible network of influences, remarkably Bedan to me. I obviously do not have space here to re-do *England and the Continent in the Eighth Century,* but I have alluded a number of times to the prominence at Charlemagne's court of one Englishman who was in many respects the intellectual heir of Gregory and of Bede. And surely one is permitted to wonder whether perhaps it was Alcuin himself who brought the magnificent "Moore Bede," now in the Cambridge University Library, to the court.[56]

Re-introducing Alcuin brings me to my third and last point. I mentioned already that it is legitimate to see Alcuin as either the author or the inspiration for the *Admonitio*. In 796 he wrote to Meginfred, a courtier, in these terms: "First, the faith is to be taught; next, the baptismal vows are to be taken; then, the gospel precepts are to be expounded. If any one of these is lacking, the listener's soul cannot enjoy salvation."[57] This is the essence of the *Admonitio* as I characterized it above. In about 793 Alcuin wrote to the Anglo-Saxon king Ethelred to remind him of his duties. He said: "Nothing defends a country better than the godliness and equity of princes and the intercession of the servants of God." He then continued: "Be rulers of the people, not robbers; shepherds, not plunderers. Obey the priests of God for they have an account to make to God how they admonish you and you, how you obey them."[58] Here again is the spirit of the *Admonitio,* but also the very heart of the Gregorian ideal of service. The *Admonitio,* I believe, represents the first and the best example of the harmonious cooperation between Alcuin and his patron Charlemagne. As Claudio Leonardi has argued, Alcuin had come to see the historic realization of the *Civitas Dei* not in the Church, as we might have expected given his English background and Bedan antecedents, but rather in the state of Charles. This was possible because Charles had defined, or had been led to define, the goal of the state as the transcending of the temporal and the human, and the transforming of all into the holy. Only Charles had the actual power and the potential universality to accomplish these lofty aims. Alcuin's contributions to the formulation of the whole vision were certainly crucial but his identification of the role of learning was unique and personal. For Augustine, learning was instrumental in that it prepared one to read the Bible and thus to be saved as an individual. For Alcuin, learning was instrumental too, but in a different sense. For the Englishman, learning led to the sanctification of the state, and a sanctified state would lead inevitably to the salvation of all its members.[59]

How do you sanctify a state? You communicate to it the one true faith, you tell it explicitly what conduct to shun, and you show it and tell it what actions to perform. You call into being, or you reform, the institutional structures necessary to implement that sanctification. That is, you publish the *Admonitio Generalis.*

Now we have a *populus Christianus* that is to be led, and taught, and preached into the kingdom of heaven by Charles along with his *sacerdotes* and *consiliares*. A consideration now of the *Libri Carolini* will enable us to see the third major component of what Michael Wallace-Hadrill once called "the public reason of the Franks."

The circumstances surrounding the production of the *Libri Carolini* are interesting, but too complicated to permit summary treatment here. We need only remind ourselves that in 787 the empress Irene held a council at Nicea to reverse the work of her iconoclast predecessors, and to restore images to their customary, honored position in the life of the faithful. Pope Hadrian had been represented at the council, but not Charlemagne or the Frankish Church. A year or two after the council, and almost certainly from Rome, Charlemagne's court received a copy of the *Acta* of Nicea II in a flawed Latin translation. Upon examining these documents it was discovered that they contained teachings on images, and on a huge array of other matters, which the Franks found objectionable. Charlemagne assembled his court theologians, under the leadership of Theodulf of Orleans, and instructed them to prepare a response to all this Byzantine perfidy. The result of their labors were the *LC*, a massive treatise – 228 quarto pages in the current *Monumenta* edition – composed in four books by Theodulf of Orleans between 790 and 793.[60] After Theodulf had drafted the text, it was submitted to intense scrutiny at the court – the most important surviving MS having more than 3,400 detectable corrections – with some of the sessions of debate and discussion taking place in Charlemagne's presence. It is hard to imagine a work that would be a better source of official thinking at Charlemagne's court in the most critical years of his reign.

A brief and outline summary of the *LC* may be helpful to readers who are not familiar with the text. Book 1 begins with an attack on the eastern emperors, and goes on to say that the Greeks misunderstand images in a fundamental way. The flaws in their reasoning are attributable to a deficient understanding of the Old Testament. Patriarch Tarasius is also severely criticized, and then more scorn is heaped on Byzantine misunderstandings of the Old Testament. Book 2 begins by carrying on the attack against Byzantine mishandling of the Bible, and then turns to a series of searing indictments of the mistakes of a number of Greek fathers and of the misuse of those fathers at Nicea. Book 3 begins with a Frankish *confessio fidei*, and then goes on to another condemnation of Tarasius which blames him for misleading his Church. Next there are several rejections of Byzantine theological errors, followed by sharp criticisms of the theological positions of a group of eastern theologians. Then we find a neat bit of ecclesiological criticism of Second Nicea, a pointed attack on Irene, and then a remarkable set of observations on what images are, what they are not, and what place they hold in the Church. The fourth and last book continues the theological reasoning begun in Book 3 but is, in a sense, more systematic and less historical, exegetical and ecclesiological – at least until the very end. Here we read that the Byzantines do not understand what an image truly is, do not understand what they are for, do not know how to establish, or to verify, evidence concerning them. The work ends with a ringing denunciation of the failure of the Byzantines to adhere to the universal traditions of the Church.

Again and again the *LC* refer to Second Nicea, and the problem of images appears in some fashion on almost every page. But I believe that Nicea provided an opportunity, and images provided an issue, that enabled the Carolingians to crystallize their thinking on a host of concerns that reached far beyond the immediate historical circumstances that had set Theodulf and his colleagues to working in the first place. The *LC* are organized around four traditions, and a discussion of each will help us see the argument of the book as a whole.

First, then, the biblical tradition. The first two books especially of the *LC* contain a series of specific, but also programmatic, condemnations of Byzantine readings of the Old Testament. In specific terms they reject a long set of passages that were adduced at Nicea in defence of images. For example, they say that Abraham did not adore the sons of Heth, and that Moses did not adore Jethro, and that Jacob did not adore Pharaoh.[61] Likewise, Jacob did not erect his pillow stone as an image, nor did he treat Joseph's cloak in this way. Jacob's staff was not an image, and neither was the Arc of the Covenant. Bezeleel did not build images, and the story of Moses and the hyacinths has no more to do with images than the tale of his bronze staff. The account of Joshua and the twelve stones does not authorize images.[62] Extensive attention is paid to the alleged misuse of the Psalms by the Byzantines. In particular, eastern interpretations of eleven psalms (4, 9, 11, 25, 29, 47, 73, 74, 84, 98, and 124) are explicitly criticized.[63] The more programmatic comments are of two kinds. In one kind, the Byzantines are hectored for failing to understand the vocabulary and grammar of the Old Testament.[64] The second kind is more serious and sustained. Again and again the Franks condemn the Byzantines for reading passages in the Old Testament literally, and for quoting those passages in connection with images when, in reality, all such passages are to be understood typologically as referring to Christ or to the Church.[65]

The Byzantines certainly did not need a lesson in typological exegesis, and at least some of the Carolingians' criticisms of the Greeks were occasioned by misunderstandings of their own prompted by the poor translation of Nicea's *acta* from which they were working. But it takes very little imagination to see that Theodulf and his associates were really giving voice to a central set of preoccupations in the Carolingian court. At just the time when the *LC* were being prepared Charlemagne's massive program of educational reform was in full swing. It would be no exaggeration to say that that program was focused directly on the Bible.[66] The whole idea of the reform was to communicate biblical truths to the people so that all might be led to salvation, and to accomplish this, as we have already seen, the right things had to be taught and to be understood. Where the Old Testament was concerned, this meant that it had to be seen as having initiated and communicated a tradition. It provided evidence for God's first compact with a chosen people. It set down God's law. And it provided very concrete examples of kings and proper kingly behavior.

One hardly knows where to begin in mentioning Carolingian evocations or appropriations of the Old Testament. Charlemagne was called David and Solomon,[67] and he called himself Josiah.[68] His chapel at Aachen was modeled in important ways on the Temple at Jerusalem, and his throne was copied from that of Solomon.[69] In the second prologue to the Salic Law and in the *Codex Carolinus*,[70] the Franks were explicitly called a "New Israel." This, it seems, was merely another way of expressing the special character of the *populus Christianus* whose existence and precise significance was coming into view just when the *LC* were being composed.

The Old Testament tradition was reformulated by the apostles and conferred upon the Church. Thus, the Bible, in the New Testament, both continues and establishes a tradition. In both respects, the Church is the repository of that tradition. Therefore, the Carolingians, in the *LC,* developed a sense of themselves as adhering loyally to what we might call ecclesiastical tradition. It is important to emphasize that this "ecclesiastical tradition" is a complement to, and not an alternative to or replacement for, the biblical tradition.

The Bible was, of course, a basic source of doctrine, and so the *LC* stress the need for doctrinal continuity. Theodulf says indeed that one must follow the teachings of the prophets, the Lord and the apostles.[71] The end of Book 2 presents an interesting set of arguments to the effect that everything needed for every possible kind of knowledge is available in Scripture.[72] Always, priority is given to the word of God.[73] But over a long period of time God's word has been interpreted, has been made accessible, has been kept inviolate by a series of authoritative teachers. Thus Book 3 contains a long series of attacks on various Greek theologians, or on the way in which those theologians were understood, or even misunderstood, at Nicea. Again and again, these theologians are accused of "novelty," an offense, largely rooted in Byzantine audacity, whose seriousness is announced already in the preface to the *LC*.[74] But the argument is not carried purely by negation. Jerome, Ambrose, Augustine and Gregory are explicitly cited as having held to the correct line in matters of faith, and there are a few more vague references to patristic traditions, and a remarkable one to the complete sufficiency of "our" Latin theologians.[75] It is perfectly true that the Carolingians sometimes were muddled about what had been said at Nicea. And on a few occasions they

admitted to being unfamiliar with texts or authors cited there. But this is
beside the point, and, as Donald Bullough has suggested, the Carolingians
may have wished to misunderstand what happened at Nicea.[76] What is clear
is that Theodulf and those who worked with him saw a straight line running
from the time of Jesus to that of Charlemagne, and as they looked back along
that line they could see that the Byzantines had at some point departed from
it.

So the Old Testament had pointed to the New, and the New had pointed
to the Church. Only the Franks had so far been faithful in all respects to
these two links in an unbroken chain of tradition. The Byzantines had fallen
away in both instances. Now, Christ himself, in his words to Peter (Matt.
16.18-19), had instituted a guarantor of his traditions, so say the *LC*. We
turn now to a third tradition, the papal, to which, according to the *LC*, the
Franks had been faithful and the Byzantines, faithless.

Very early the *LC* set about emphasizing the importance of communion
with Rome. At the end of the fifth chapter of Book 1 we read that whenever a doctrinal question arises the Roman Church is to be consulted. The
following chapter is the most rigorously papalist in the whole treatise. It
makes three very simple, direct arguments: The Roman Church has from
the beginning been set before all other Churches; only books used in Rome
and teachings that hold authority there are to be admitted; and although
many people have at some time broken from Rome's communion, the Franks
never have. Indeed, they struggle mightily to bring new peoples, such as the
Saxons, into the Roman fold.[77] Elsewhere in the text we find that, on one
occasion, the teaching authority of Pope Sylvester is affirmed,[78] while, on
another occasion, some debating points are scored against the Byzantines by
pointing out that even so great a scholar as St. Jerome did not hesitate to
turn for instruction to Pope Damasus.[79] And Pope Gregory I, a great Frankish favorite in all circumstances, is referred to repeatedly. The position of
the papacy as the culmination and guarantee of ecclesiastical traditions can
be set off neatly against the allegedly irregular and schismatic situation of
Patriarch Tarasius.[80] The remarks in the *LC* about the papacy are in perfect
agreement with what the text says about biblical and ecclesiastical traditions. A critical set of developments began in ancient Israel, and continued
into Charlemagne's Francia. That set did not include the Byzantines.

One final line of historical development is worked out in the *LC*. It might
be called Christian-imperial. The *LC* talk fairly often about rulership, and
virtually everything that is said involves implicit and explicit comparisons of
good and bad rulership. The Byzantine rulers, often derisively called "kings,"
are called arrogant and uncharitable (i.e lacking in *caritas*). The point of
these criticisms is to drive home the distinction between the Byzantines and
the Franks, whose royal theory insisted that they be humble, loving servants

of God and his people. The Greeks are taxed for having the temerity to refer to their acts as *divalia,* for claiming that God ruled with them, and for asserting equality with the apostles.[81] Charlemagne ruled by God's grace, ruled at his pleasure and as his servant, and never dreamed of speaking of himself in divine terms. In this connection, the *LC* fire off one of their deadliest darts. They say that the imperial conduct of the Byzantines makes them like the pagan Romans who were the heirs of Babylon.[82] Small wonder, then, that the emperors of the east have misled their people. Charlemagne will have to answer to God for the people entrusted to his care. He will have to lay down an account just as the kings of the Old Testament had to do.

By returning to the kings of the Old Testament we have closed the circle and can now conclude. The *LC* are a masterfully designed strategy in the Carolingian fight for history. They were produced in the court of a king who in 789 compared himself to Josiah in his responsibility to teach and to admonish his people. Persons at that court also called Charlemagne David, who struggled for the Lord's causes, and Solomon, to whom the Lord had given wisdom. Charlemagne ruled over the Franks, who were called a "New Israel." The *LC* are an elegant metahistory that can in every way bear favorable comparison with the more famous works of Eusebius and Orosius and even, in a way, with Augustine's. They are a metahistory that seeks to locate the Franks in their own time, but also in all time. This is why I insisted at the outset that Nicea and images merely provided an opportunity for deeper reflections on larger themes.

Can anyone be surprised that a few years after the *LC* were written Charlemagne was crowned emperor? This magnificent book had already prepared for that event by demonstrating that God's covenant with Abraham had been communicated to the Church, preserved by the popes, and transferred to the Franks. The Byzantines, who alone in the late eighth century could have competed with the Franks on grounds of spiritual and historical universalism, had to be written out of history, as it were. This was done to them in two ways. First they were made the object of almost unspeakable scorn. They and their teachings were called arrogant, contemptible, damnable, laughable, stupid, foolish, silly, inadequate, inappropriate, incautious, superficial – I could go on and on. At Byzantium a person was rendered ineligible for high office by physical mutilation. The Franks rendered the Byzantines ineligible for historical participation by verbal mutilation. Second, and more significantly, the *LC* neatly set aside all possibility that the Byzantines could be regarded as the heirs of Israel, of the Old Testament, of apostolic traditions, of the ancient councils, of the Roman papacy, and of the Christian Roman Empire. When Theodulf laid down his quill, all of history had been made to point to the very court in which he had been working.

What is the argument of the *LC*? It is a simple one that goes like this: Abraham was a Frank, and David was a Carolingian. But the treatise was, as Walter Schmandt said, a *Staatsschrift*,[83] and as such it contained no less than the fullest single expression of the ideological program of the court of Charlemagne.

At this point there is no need to engage in a lengthy commentary on the *capitula* from the great meeting at Frankfurt in 794.[84] It suffices to remark that those decrees serve in a remarkable way as a synthesis and summation of all that had been happening in official circles in the Frankish world for almost a decade. Years ago Ganshof devoted a penetrating study to the synod and assembly of Frankfurt.[85] I agree with almost everything he said, and would add only the sense of pattern that I detect in Frankfurt's relationship to the program that had been evolving since at least 785. The *capitula* begin with an evocation of apostolic authority. Nothing is more to be expected. Here is made explicit the Carolingian concern for the *norma rectitudinis,* the overwhelming sense that there was a right way to do things, and that that way was usually to be found in Rome. Then the decrees go on to condemn Adoptionism and Second Nicea. Here we find that characteristic sense that the faith is primary and must be kept pure. The following decree handles the rebellious Bavarian duke, Tassilo. Here, if I have read things correctly, we find a practical implementation of the *populus Christianus* concept I mentioned earlier. The very next *capitulum* forbids selling grain at a profit, or hoarding it, during famines. This is precisely the kind of specific enactment that would be demanded by the moral, ministerial program enunciated in the *Admonitio.* The remaining *capitula* are, for the most part, very precise and specific, but almost all are, in either substantive or thematic terms, follow-ups to the *capitula* of the *Admonitio.* The Council of Frankfurt was the obvious counterpart to the Council of Nicea held seven years before. Traditions were affirmed; no novelties were introduced. Charlemagne exercised his roles, as spelled out in the *Admonitio,* of visitation, admonition and correction; he made no vain and diabolical attacks upon the Church, its teachings, and its people. He showed the courage of David and the wisdom of Solomon.

In other words, then, what I see between 785 or so and 794 is the development at the court of Charlemagne of a public ideology for the Carolingian realm. People were assembled, values were discussed and a select body of ideas was given concrete form in a major set of public acts. Not before this time, and not again afterwards, not even around the coronation of 800, did the court of Charlemagne do so much that was so consistent. The many peoples of the *regnum Francorum* were redefined as a single *populus Christianus.* The leaders of that "Christian people" articulated their resposibilities not in terms of ethnic or military leadership, but rather in terms of biblical and ecclesiastical concepts of peace, love and justice. Finally, an historical doctrine was elaborated according to which the Franks were the realization and culmination of a tradition that had its rise in the selection of Abraham as the patriarch of the first chosen people.

Charlemagne, then, had traded brigandage for justice. Of what did this justice consist? It consisted of three inextricably interlocked notions. First, faith had to be correct, free of error, historically confirmed, widely disseminated and universally embraced. Second, this faith had to infuse all public institutions. It had to define them, and to give them their sense of meaning and purpose. Third, when faith had been taught well and widely, and when institutions had been put in place to sustain and to expand that faith, then individuals would be reformed, would be re-made, would be saved. Salvation may seem to us an odd goal for government, but for those around Charlemagne it had come to seem that a government that did not set out to save men's souls had no reason for being. This idea of justice was very Roman, but it came neither from Cicero nor from the law. Rather, it came from a Roman called Gregory who, like Charles, was thought by some of his contemporaries, and by many people later, to deserve the epithet *Magnus.*

Notes

1. *Vita Karoli,* c. 24, ed. Louis Halphen (Paris, 1938), 72. Michel Rouche ("The Early Middle Ages in the West," in Paul Veyne ed., *A History of Private Life* 1, *From Pagan Rome to Byzantium,* trans. Arthur Goldhammer [Cambridge, MA, 1987], 450) captures the issues well when he writes that to Charlemagne "the Ciceronian adage, 'No state without justice,' with its Augustinian gloss, 'no state without God,' the sole teacher of righteousness, signified that a pagan state was a contradiction in terms."

2. Augustine, *The City of God* 4.4, trans. Henry Bettenson (London, 1972), 139.

3. "Plunder and Tribute in the Carolingian Empire," *Transactions of the Royal Historical Society,* 5th series, 35 (1985): 75-94.

4. This is hardly the place for a comprehensive assessment of Carolingian political thought generally, or of Charlemagne's ideas specifically. A superb introduction is provided by Janet L. Nelson, "Kingship and Empire," in J. H. Burns, ed., *The Cambridge History of Medieval Political Thought* (Cambridge, 1988), 211-51. An excellent analysis of some key concepts is Sybille Mahl, *Quadriga Virtutum: Die Kardinaltugenden in der Geistesgeschichte der Karolingerzeit* (Cologne, 1969). The fundamental study of the relevant sources remains Hans Hubert Anton, *Fürstenspiegel und Herrscherethos in der Karolingerzeit,* Bonner historische Forschungen 32 (Bonn, 1968), esp. 45-131. The essential background is surveyed in Eugen Ewig, "Zum christlichen Königsgedanken im Frühmittelalter," in Theodor Mayer, ed., *Das Königtum: Seine geistigen und rechtlichen Grundlagen,* Vorträge und Forschungen 3 (Lindau-Konstanz, 1956), 7-73. For a spirited presentation of a view which I consider insupportable, namely that Charlemagne's piety remained militantly Germanic, see Adolf Waas, "Karls des Grossen Frömmigkeit," *Historische Zeitschrift* 203 (1966): 265-79.

5. The anecdote dates from 1973. For the article see *The Carolingians and the Frankish Monarchy,* trans. Janet Sondheimer (Ithaca, 1971), 256-60. It first appeared in 1947. I do not know, or do not remember, when the encounter between Ganshof and Calmette occurred.

6. Ganshof's most pointed observations can be found in his article "Charlemagne," in idem, *The Carolingians and the Frankish Monarchy,* 17-27 (delivered as an address to the Medieval Academy of America in 1948 and published in 1949). At p. 17 Ganshof said he aimed to provide "a broad outline of his personality as a statesman." Donald Bullough's reservations can be most conveniently found in his *The Age of Charlemagne,* 2nd ed. (London, 1973), 11-12. He quotes the no less formidable Michael Wallace-Hadrill who said, "His personality as a statesman does not and probably never did exist."

7. Riché, "Le renouveau culturel à la cour de Pépin III," *Francia* 2 (1974): 59-70. Hubert, "Les prémisses de la Renaissance carolingienne au temps de Pépin III," ibid., 49-58. The most recent and important studies of ecclesiastical developments are E. Ewig, "Beobachtungen zur Entwicklung der fränkischen Reichskirche unter Chrodegang von Metz," *Frühmittelalterliche Studien* 2 (1968): 67-77 and Josef Semmler, "Pippin III und die fränkischen Klöster," *Francia* 3 (1975): 88-146. Bullough shares my reservations about the validity of comparing Pepin's and Charlemagne's reigns on even terms: "*Aula Renovata:* The Carolingian Court Before the Aachen Palace," *Proceedings of the British Academy* 71 (1985): 269-71.

8. See my "Louis the Pious and the Frontiers of the Frankish Realm," in Peter Godman and Roger Collins, eds., *Charlemagne's Heir: New Perspectives on the Reign of Louis the Pious* (Oxford, 1990), 333-47.

9. Quoted by Richard E. Sullivan, *The Coronation of Charlemagne: What Did It Signify?* (Boston, 1959), xv.

10. Engelbert Mühlbacher, *Deutsche Geschichte unter den Karolingern* (Stuttgart, 1896; repr. Darmstadt, 1959), 84-318; Arthur Kleinclausz, *Charlemagne* (Paris, 1934; repr. 1977); Louis Halphen, *Charlemagne et l'empire carolingien* (Paris, 1947; repr. 1968), 57-194.

11. The article is cited in n.5 above. Another valuable study is contained in a pamphlet that did not circulate widely: *Charlemagne: Sa personnalité, son héritage* (Brussels, 1965). Other articles that adopt a chronological approach are included in *The Carolingians and the Frankish Monarchy*. Two others that retain their fundamental significance are "Une crise dans le règne de Charlemagne: Les années 778 et 779," in *Mélanges Charles Gilliard* (Lausanne, 1944) and "Observations sur le synode de Francfort de 794," in *Miscellanea A. de Meyer* (Louvain, 1946).

12. *The Republic of St. Peter: The Birth of the Papal State, 680-825* (Philadelphia, 1984), 138-83.

13. One study, "*Aula Renovata*," 269-301, is cited above in n.7. The other is "*Albuinus deliciosus Karoli regis:* Alcuin of York and the Shaping of the Early Carolingian Court," in L. Fenske et al., eds., *Institutionen, Kultur und Gesellschaft: Festschrift für Josef Fleckenstein zum 65. Geburtstag* (Sigmaringen, 1984), 72-92.

14. For details on the Godescalc Evangelistary see Jean Hubert, Jean Porcher and W. F. Volbach, *Carolingian Art* (London, 1970), 75-78 and for general context see Joachim Gaehde and Florentine Mütherich, *Carolingian Painting* (London, 1977), 7-11 with plates 1-3, 32-35. See also the comments by Lawrence Nees in his article in this volume: "The Originality of Early Medieval Artists," at n.30.

15. For general details see Kenneth John Conant, *Carolingian and Romanesque Architecture, 800-1200,* 2nd ed. (Harmondsworth, 1966), 43-51. For Aachen it still suffices to refer to Ludwig Falkenstein, "Zwischenbilanz zur aachener Pfalzenforschung," *Zeitschrift der aachener Geschichtsverein* 80 (1970): 7-71.

16. *Codex Carolinus,* no. 89, in Wilhelm Gundlach, ed., *Monumenta Germaniae Historica* (henceforth abbreviated as *MGH*), *Epistolarum* 3, *Epistolae Merowingici et Karolini Aevi* 1 (Berlin, 1892), 626. It has always been assumed that the dispatch of this sacramentary should be dated 784/5, but Bullough has made a convincing case for redating Hadrian's letter to 786/7: "Ethnic History and the Carolingians: An Alternative Reading of Paul the Deacon's *Historia Langobardorum,*" in Christopher Holdsworth and T. P. Wiseman, eds., *The Inheritance of Historiography, 350-900,* Exeter Studies in History 12 (Exeter, 1986), 102 n.6. The text has been edited, with abundant commentary and notes, by Jean Deshusses, *Le sacramentaire grégorien,* 2nd ed., 3 vols. (Freiburg, 1979).

17. See the letter by means of which Charlemagne announced the work: No. 30, in Alfred Boretius, ed., *MGH, Legum Sectio* 2, *Capitularia Regum Francorum* (henceforth abbreviated as *Cap.*) 1 (Hanover, 1881), 80-1. There is not yet a satisfactory edition of this critical text. See Rosamond McKitterick, *The Frankish Church and the Carolingian Reforms* (London, 1977), 102-104, 102 n.3. The version most frequently referred to is *PL* 95.1159-1584.

18. *Epistula ad regem Karolum de monasterio sancti Benedicti directa et a Paolo dictata,* ed. Kassius Hallinger, *Corpus Consuetudinum Monasticarum* 1 (Siegburg, 1963), 157-75, esp. 159-60. See also C.H. Lawrence, *Medieval Monasticism,* 2nd ed. (London, 1989), 22.

19. No. 22, *MGH, Cap.* 1.52-57. See Hubert Mordek, "Kirchenrechtliche Autoritäten im Frühmittelalter," in Peter Classen, ed., *Recht und Schrift im Mittelalter,* Vorträge und Forschungen 23 (Sigmaringen, 1977), 23-48.

20. Philip Grierson and Mark Blackburn, *Medieval European Coinage, Vol. 1, The Early Middle Ages* (Cambridge, 1986), 205-10, esp. 208-209.

21. Ganshof, *Frankish Institutions under Charlemagne,* trans. Bryce and Mary Lyon (New York, 1968), 23-26.

22. See n.12 above.

23. No. 23, c. 18, *MGH, Cap.* 1.63.

24. No. 24, *MGH, Cap.* 1.65-6.

25. No. 25, c. 1, *MGH, Cap.* 1.67. Additional details concerning the rebellion, which seems to have been centered in Thuringia, to have been led by a certain Hardrad, and to have involved counts and others of high status, are found in narrative sources, such as: *Annales regni Francorum,* ed. Friedrich Kurze, *MGH, SSRG* 6, *sub anno 785,* 70; *Annales laurissenses, MGH, Scriptores* 1.32; *Annales sancti Nazariani,* ibid., 41-43. The fullest discussion of the rebellion and the subsequent oaths is Karl Brunner, *Oppositionelle Gruppen im Karolingerreich,* Veröffentlichen des Instituts für Österreichische Geschichtsforschung 25 (Vienna, 1979), 47-52.

26. Ganshof, "Charlemagne's Use of the Oath," in *The Carolingians and the Frankish Monarchy,* 111-24, esp. 112-13.

27. *MGH, Cap.* 1.68-70. This is not the place to argue out the issue, but I am inclined to favor a date nearer to 782 than to 785.

28. *Annales regni Francorum,* ed. Kurze, *sub anno 781,* 56.

29. Still valuable here is Gustav Eiten, *Das Unterkönigtum im Reiche der Merowinger und Karolinger,* Heidelberger Abhandlungen zur mittleren und neueren Geschichte 18 (Heidelberg, 1907), 18ff., 35ff.

30. See n.12 above.

31. *Annales regni Francorum,* ed. Kurze, *sub anno 786,* 72.

32. The story of Tassilo's fall has been told many times, for example by Rosamond McKitterick, *The Frankish Kingdoms under the Carolingians* (London, 1983), 66-68.

33. Noble, *Republic of St. Peter,* 176-78.

34. I cite the relevant literature in the study referred to in n.8 above.

35. Paulinus of Aquileia, *Libellus adversus Elipandum,* in A. Werminghoff, ed., *MGH, Legum Sectio 3, Concilia 2, Concilia aevi Karolini 2* (Hanover, 1896), 142; *Admonitio Generalis,* c. 62, *MGH, Cap.* 1.58. *Populus Christianus* also begins to turn up regularly in semi-official narrative sources such as *Annales regni Francorum,* ed. Kurze, *sub anno 791,* 88.

36. Alcuin, *Ep.* 41, in Ernst Dümmler, ed., *MGH, Epistolarum 4, Epistolae Karolini Aevi* (henceforth abbreviated as *Epp.*) 2 (Berlin, 1895), 84.

37. For the text, *MGH, Cap.* 1.52-62; for King's translation see his *Charlemagne: Translated Sources* (Lancaster, 1987), 209-20.

38. Hubert Mordek and Gerhard Schmitz, "Neue Kapitularien und Kapitulariensammlungen," *Deutsches Archiv* 43 (1987): 361-439.

39. In this I follow Josef Fleckenstein, *Die Bildungsreform Karls des Grossen als Verwirklichung der Norma Rectitudinis* (Bigge-Ruhr, 1953), 71-73.

40. *Recherches sur les capitulaires* (Paris, 1958).

41. Hincmar, *De ordine palatii,* c. 6, Thomas Gross and Rudolf Schieffer, eds., *MGH, Fontes iuris Germanici antiqui* 3 (Hanover, 1980), 82-90.

42. On capitularies in general and consensus see: Hannig, *Consensus Fidelium: Frühfeudale Interpretationen des Verhältnisses von Königtum und Adel am Beispiel des Frankenreiches,* Monographien zur Geschichte des Mittelalters 27 (Stuttgart, 1982); Nelson, "Legislation and Consensus in the Reign of Charles the Bald," in Patrick Wormald, ed., *Ideal and Reality in Frankish and Anglo-Saxon Society* (Oxford, 1983), 222-27; Schmitz, "The Capitulary Legislation of Louis the Pious," in Godman and Collins, eds., *Charlemagne's Heir,* 425-436 (an abbreviated version of the German original published in *Deutsches Archiv* 42 (1986): 471-516). Additional, important studies that have influenced my thinking are: Reinhard Schneider, "Zur rechtlichen Bedeutung der Kapitularientexte," *Deutsches Archiv* 23 (1967): 273-94; idem, "Schriftlichkeit und Mundlichkeit im Bereich der Kapitularien," in Classen, ed., *Recht und Schrift,* 257-80; Dieter Hägermann, "Zur Entstehung der Kapitularien," in Waldemar Schlogl and Peter Herde, eds., *Festschrift für Peter Acht* (Kallmütz, 1976), 12-27.

43. *Admonitio Generalis, Prol., MGH, Cap.* 1.52.

44. Friedrich-Karl Schiebe, "Alcuin und die *Admonitio Generalis," Deutsches Archiv* 14 (1958): 221-29; Bullough, "Alcuin and the Kingdom of Heaven: Liturgy, Theology and the Carolingian Age," in Uta-Renate Blumenthal, ed., *Carolingian Essays* (Washington, 1983), 22 and *"Aula Renovata,"* 294. McKitterick, *Frankish Church,* 1 n.2 dismisses Schiebe's arguments but does not say why she does so. I have profited from stimulating discussions of these problems with Katy Cubitt and Patrick Wormald.

45. See above n.19.

46. *Codex Carolinus,* no. 3, *MGH, Epp.* 1.479-87.

47. No. 29, *MGH, Cap.* 1.79.

48. This is the central thesis of Fleckenstein's *Norma Rectitudinis* (above, n.39).

49. Patrick Wormald, *"Lex Scripta* and *Verbum Regis:* Legislation and Germanic Kingship From Euric to Cnut," in Peter Sawyer and Ian Wood, eds., *Early Medieval Kingship* (Leeds, 1977), 132.

50. *Norma Rectitudinis,* 52.

51. Godman, *Poetry of the Carolingian Renaissance* (London, 1985), no. 6, pp. 112-18 (with a beautiful English translation, pp. 113-19). Angilbert does not actually use the phrase *rex doctus*. This is a term of learned discussion bearing upon the image of a king who is imagined to be learned and to be the patron of learning. See Godman, *Poets and Emperors: Frankish Politics and Carolingian Poetry* (Oxford, 1987), 1-37, 65-68. Its first occurrence may be in the exchange of poems between Peter of Pisa and Paul the Deacon: Godman, *Poetry*, nos. 2, 3, pp. 82-89.

52. Godman, *Poetry*, nos. 7, 15, pp. 118-20, 150-62. Alcuin's letters are also full of this language. For the poem from the Godescalc Evangelistary see Ernst Dümmler, ed., *MGH, Poetarum Latinorum Medii Aevi* 1, *Poetae Latini Aevi Carolini* 1 (Berlin, 1881), 94-95; and in this volume, Nees, "Originality," at n.30.

53. Godman, *Poets and Emperors*, 38-92 passim, esp. 46ff. One of Godman's key observations (47), which I find completely persuasive, is that all of these writings "responded to Charlemagne's personal initiative and reflected his public interests."

54. Fleckenstein, *Norma Rectitudinis*, 24-5, 40-45, 67-69, 73-75; Ewig, "Königsgedanken," (above, n.4) 3-4, 58-63; Wallace-Hadrill, *Early Germanic Kingship* (Oxford, 1971); Robert Folz, *The Coronation of Charlemagne*, trans. J. E. Anderson (London, 1974), 77ff.

55. For example by Folz, *Imperial Coronation*, 77; Wolfgang Fritze, "*Universalis Gentium Confessio*: Formeln, Träger und Wege universalmissionarischen Denkens im 7. Jahrhundert," *Frühmittelalterliche Studien* 3 (1969): 78-130, at 106-13. On Gregory himself there are some good words in Robert Markus, "The Latin Fathers," in Burns, ed., *Cambridge History of Medieval Political Thought*, 116-22.

56. Bernhard Bischoff, "Die Hofbibliothek Karls des Grossen," in Helmut Beumann, ed., *Karl der Grosse* 2 (Düsseldorf, 1966), 56.

57. Alcuin, *Ep.* 111, *MGH, Epp.* 2.160.

58. Alcuin, *Ep.* 16, *MGH, Epp.* 2.42-44.

59. "Alcuino e la scuola palatina: le ambizioni di una cultura unitaria," *Settimane di studio del centro di studi sull'alto medioevo* 27 (1981): 459-96.

60. The fundamental studies of the *Libri Carolini* are by Ann Freeman: "Theodulf of Orleans and the *Libri Carolini*," *Speculum* 32 (1957): 663-705; "Further Studies in the *Libri Carolini*, I and II," *Speculum* 40 (1965): 203-89; "Further Studies in the *Libri Carolini*, III. The Marginal Notes in Vaticanus latinus 7207," *Speculum* 46 (1971): 597-612; "Carolingian Orthodoxy and the Fate of the *Libri Carolini*," *Viator* 16 (1985): 65-108;

"Theodulf of Orléans and the Psalm Citations of the 'Libri Carolini'," *Revue Bénédictine* 97 (1987): 195-224; "Additions and Corrections to the *Libri Carolini;* Links with Alcuin and the Adoptionist Controversy," in Sigrid Krämer and Michael Bernhard, eds., *Scire litteras: Forschungen zum mittelalterlichen Geistesleben,* Abhandlungen der bayerische Akademie der Wissenschaften, philosophisch-historische Klasse, neue Folge 99 (Munich, 1988), 159-69. Valuable too, and sadly neglected, is Walther Schmandt, *Studien zu den Libri Carolini* (Mainz, 1966). I am grateful to Paul Meyvaert for bringing this study to my attention. Luitpold Wallach made many valuable contributions to *Libri Carolini* studies but never abandoned his belief that Alcuin was the principal author of the text. His papers are conveniently collected in his *Diplomatic Studies in Latin and Greek Documents from the Carolingian Age* (Ithaca, 1977). Between them Freeman and Wallach cite the older literature very fully.

61. H. Bastgen, ed., *Libri Carolini sive Carolini Magni capitulare de imaginibus, MGH Legum sectio 3, Concilia 2, supplementum* (Hanover, 1924) (= *LC*), 1.9, pp. 26-28. A revised edition of the *LC* by Ann Freeman is forthcoming.

62. *LC* 1.10, Bastgen 28-29; 1.12, Bastgen 31-32; 1.13, Bastgen 32-33; 1.15, Bastgen 34-37; 1.16, Bastgen 37-39; 1.17, Bastgen 39-42; 1.18, Bastgen 42-44.

63. *LC* 1.23, Bastgen 50-52; 1.25, Bastgen 53-54; 1.26, Bastgen 54-55; 1.28, Bastgen 56-57; 1.29, Bastgen 57-59; 1.30, Bastgen 60; 2.1-2, Bastgen 63-64; 2.3, Bastgen 64-65; 2.5, Bastgen 66-68; 2.7-8, Bastgen 69. I am inclined to wonder if so much attention was paid to the Psalms because of their role in the public and private prayer of the western Church.

64. *LC* 1.9, Bastgen 26-28; 1.29, Bastgen 57-59; 2.1, Bastgen 63.

65. *LC* 1.5, Bastgen 18-19; 1.15, Bastgen 34-37; 1.17, Bastgen 39-42; 1.18, Bastgen 42-44; 1.19, Bastgen 44-45; 1.20, Bastgen 48. Several of the passages cited above in n.63 bear on these issues as well. Indeed, they come up again and again in Bks. 1 and 2.

66. On biblical studies generally see John J. Contreni, "Carolingian Biblical Studies," in Blumenthal, ed., *Carolingian Essays,* 71-98. The studies of Ewig ("Königsgedanken") and Fleckenstein (*Norma Rectitudinis*) (above, nn.4, 39 resp.) do justice to the place of *sacra scriptura* in Carolingian political thought and education. The subject is not controversial and references could be piled up endlessly.

67. The fullest discussion of David imagery remains Walter Mohr, *Die karolingische Reichsidee,* Aevum Christianum 5 (Münster, 1962), 6-38. Godman, *Poets and Emperors,* ch. 2 has much relevant material.

68. In the *Admonitio Generalis, Prol., MGH, Cap.* 1.54.

69. The most stimulating assessment of Aachen remains, in my view, Heinrich Fichtenau, "Byzanz und die Pfalz zu Aachen," *Mitteilungen des Instituts für Österreichisches Geschichtsforschung* 59 (1951): 1-54. On the throne see: Horst Appuhn, "Zum Thron Karls des Großen," *Aachener Kunstblätter* 24/5 (1962/3): 127-36; Roderich Schmidt, "Zur Geschichte des fränkischen Königsthrons," *Frühmittelalterliche Studien* 2 (1968): 45-66.

70. *Lex salica,* in K. A. Eckhardt, ed., *MGH, Leges, Legum Sectio* 1, *Legum Nationum Germanicarum* 4.2 (Hanover, 1969), 1-9. *Codex Carolinus,* no. 39, *MGH, Epp.* 1.552.

71. *LC* 2.25, Bastgen 84-85.

72. *LC* 2.30-31, Bastgen 92-102, esp. 95-96. A key source here must have been Augustine: Peter Brown, *Augustine of Hippo* (Berkeley, 1969), 259-69, esp. 263-64.

73. This theme is developed in interesting ways by Rosamond McKitterick, "Text and Image in the Carolingian World," in idem, ed., *The Uses of Literacy in the Early Middle Ages* (Cambridge, 1990), 297-318.

74. *LC, Praef.,* Bastgen 4.

75. *LC, Praef.,* Bastgen 4-5; 2.17, Bastgen 76-77.

76. *The Age of Charlemagne,* 111.

77. *LC* 1.5-6, Bastgen 19-22.

78. *LC* 2.13, Bastgen 73.

79. *LC* 1.5, Bastgen 21.

80. Tarasius comes in for repeated criticism and abuse: e.g. *LC* 1.20, Bastgen 45, 46; 3.2, Bastgen 108-109; 3.3, Bastgen 110-13; 3.5, Bastgen 115-16; etc.

81. *LC* 1.1, Bastgen 8-10, 12; 1.2, Bastgen 12-14; 1.3, Bastgen 14; 1.4, Bastgen 16-18. The terminology used by the Byzantines was traditionally Roman. Did the Franks know this and deliberately misrepresent the Byzantine position, or were they ignorant of the actual significance of, for example, the emperors calling themselves *divos* and their acts *divalia*? I suspect that this is a case of what Bullough sees as willful misunderstanding. For the terminology see Otto Hiltbrunner, "Die Heiligkeit des Kaisers," *Frühmittelalterliche Studien* 2 (1968): 1-30.

82. *LC* 3.15, Bastgen 135.

83. *Studien,* 1 (above, n.60).

84. For its decrees: *MGH, Cap.* 1.73-78. An outstanding recent discussion of Frankfurt is Wilfried Hartmann, *Die Synoden der Karolingerzeit im Frankreich und in Italien* (Paderborn, 1989), 105-15.

85. See above, n.11.

THE ORIGINALITY OF EARLY MEDIEVAL ARTISTS

Lawrence Nees

The topic of the originality of early medieval artists is vast in scope as well as difficult in terms of both method and material, and is certainly too many-faceted for treatment in the span of a single paper. Yet the topic has seemed to me to demand renewed attention,[1] and attracted my attention not only because it bears upon research interests of long standing on my part, but also because it addresses interests closely related to the broader humanistic issues and procedures that first attracted me to the study of medieval art. Thus what I have to offer here may have rather too much the quality of a confession, but since the questions at issue involve the individual, personal and occasionally self-revelatory element of early medieval art, perhaps the confessional element of my presentation at least embodies a certain symmetry between subject and object, while at the same time attaching itself to an Augustinian prototype in good early medieval fashion.

There is a more proximate anecdotal cause for my choice of topic, since I was asked to provide a title for this presentation shortly after reading two articles in the 1988 issues of *The Art Bulletin,* articles which take sharply differing approaches to the relationship between artist and prior pictorial model in the creation of early medieval art. The first article, by Herbert Kessler, stated that "it was only very late [in the Middle Ages] that the 'idea' of an individual 'artist' with an independent, determining imagination emerged and then only as part of the process leading to the Renaissance."[2] The careful reader should note that Kessler explicitly states only that the articulated "idea" and not the actual reality of artists with independent imaginations was lacking in the early Middle Ages, and indeed he has himself recently provided a fine contextual analysis of an example of iconographic innovation in the early Middle Ages.[3] Nevertheless, in his programmatic article he argues for a very restricted dimension of artistic imagination in real practice, observing that during the early medieval period

> in manuscript illumination, where the scribal mentality reinforced the principle of accurate copying, art was principally an act of duplication. Although personal traits and even small intentional alterations always appear, the goal was generally to come as close as possible to reproducing the model.[4]

To be sure I have taken these quotations out of their broader context and thereby sharpened them, but I hope I have not distorted the essential emphasis on the relatively passive and reproductive role of the early medieval artist in comparison to the power of pictorial traditions and models.

The second article to which I refer is by Jeffrey Anderson, in which he observes that even in the case of the Byzantine Psalters with illustrations in the margins, long regarded as a classic field for the deployment of what art historians have called philological or recensional analysis, that is, the establishment of a chain of copies descending from a single archetype, rigid recensional analysis simply does not work. Anderson observes that

> not one of the three ninth-century examples ... is the copy of another... The illustrations of these books cannot be compared with the copying of biblical or classical texts. Absent is the one prerequisite for establishing a recension: conscientious adherence to the model. Accuracy to a single collection of images did not guide any of the illuminators... Virtually all of them consciously added and modified, presumably with some purpose in mind.[5]

The contrast between these two recent general statements assessing the relationship between the copying of artistic models and what Kessler calls the "independent determining imagination" of individual artists could hardly be more clear and sharp.[6] Manifestly the originality of early medieval artists is a current problem deserving renewed attention, and ought to begin in good scholastic fashion with a definition of the critical term. As is so often the case, the dictionary is not very helpful in this regard. The *Oxford English Dictionary* defines the word "original" first as "the fact or attribute of being primary or first-hand; authenticity, genuineness," second as "the quality of being independent of and different from anything that has appeared before; novelty or freshness of style or character," and third "as an attribute of persons: exhibition of original thought or action; the character of independently exercising one's own faculties; the power of originating new or fresh ideas or methods."[7] All of these definitions fall short of addressing the central notion of originality as that term is employed in the modern scholarly jargon of art historians, a topic whose proper investigation would constitute an immense historiographical undertaking. The term is, in the fullest sense of the word, problematic. To the dictionary denotations of originality, art historians have commonly added connotations of self-conscious intention, and of a significant contribution to historical progress. The original artist not only displays new and fresh ideas, but is aware of and proud of the novelty, and contributes important novelties upon which other artists will eventually build a broader new direction in the general development of art. An original artist is generally thought to be influential rather than merely idiosyncratic. Thus the originality of early medieval artists may be approached under three headings, creativity itself, self-esteem and self-consciousness, and historical development. I propose to treat the three headings in reverse order, so as to conclude with the fundamental question of creativity, upon which the others depend.

Originality and Historical Development

Until very recently, the now suddenly problematic notion that art had a history distinct from our critical elaboration of it was taken for granted,[8] and the major critical debates focused upon the mechanism by which that historical development was driven. Although often given the central role in later periods, individual artists were not regarded as important developmental engines during the early Middle Ages. I by no means wish to propose a return to the old heroic model of the history of art as the product of individual "geniuses" who created unique masterpieces and served as the heroes of art history, nor to propose the adoption of that increasingly discredited notion for the early medieval period.[9] The deficiencies of such a model were recognized more than a century ago, and the "original genius" model clearly could never have been made to work for early medieval art, because of the dearth of the necessary biographical sources. Indeed the limitations of the biograpical approach helped drive early scholars to define the Middle Ages as a time of poor artistic achievement precisely because of those scholars' relative ignorance of individual artistic personalities - a vicious circle.

Scholars of the late nineteenth and early twentieth century concerned with the early medieval tradition attempted to make a virtue of necessity by using the undeniable plain fact of profound artistic change and "development" during the period even in the absence of Michelangelesque geniuses to rebut the methodological premises upon which the biographical, heroic model rested. In his famous 1901 study of late Roman and early medieval art, Alois Riegl expounded his very influential thesis of autonomous transformation of artistic style for purely artistic reasons without reference to external factors such as individual choices. For Riegl, although the individual element of artistic creation is undeniable, artistic development follows an inherent suprapersonal necessity which he termed the *Kunstwollen*.[10] The success of Riegl's theory in making all art, including the then much-maligned "barbaric" and unclassical art of the early medieval period,[11] of equal historical value and interest carried with it the corollary that the already very difficult task of isolating and evaluating the conscious intention and achievement of the early medieval artist was a trivial matter, a waste of time and effort. Early medieval art thus became a kind of laboratory for the study of the non-individual in art, and the fundamental and decisive question became not "what did the artist intend, or accomplish, or (even) do?" but rather "where is the work of art located in a continuous artistic development that can be reconstructed by the historian?"

From such a question and from such a historiographical tradition stems the abstract scheme of the development of early medieval art published by Charles Rufus Morey in 1924 (fig.1).[12] If, as we see here, Byzantine art is descended as a whole from its ancestors, the Alexandrian and Asiatic branches of the Hellenistic tradition, and the Carolingian Reims style was sired by Alexandrian Impressionism out of Latin Illusionism, as it were, then the personal situation and accomplishments of the Carolingian artists are trivial and tangential details that may be of great aesthetic merit but possess scant historical significance. At the same time, even very innovative and creative artistic achievements that do not appear to lead anywhere in the developments defined by our own omniscient hindsight have no interest or value whatsoever, and can scarcely be defined as "original," since originality has in fact been defined with reference not to the past but to the future.

Although it seems to me that the premises upon which Morey's ideas are based continue to dominate much art historical research, which has by no means deposed the concept of development from its methodologically privileged throne, the schematic outlines of his genealogical tree seem today bizarre. However, this conception was quite influential during the period prior to the second world war, and was even transferred to other historical areas. Morey's own student Alfred Barr drew a similarly schematic developmental genealogy for the great "Cubism and Abstract Art" exhibition held at the Museum of Modern Art in 1936, a chart reproduced on the back cover of the catalogue and prominently displayed as a major wall poster in the exhibition (fig.2).[13] The notion that Futurism, for example, is a product of Neo-impressionism and Cubism with a dash of machine aesthetic is obviously derived by Barr from the historiographical methodology of his teacher Morey. Yet in the case of modern art we all know only too well that Marinetti had a large and arguably decisive personal role in the Futurist movement, as did Picasso and Braque in the "invention" of Cubism, and so forth. Indeed at the top of Barr's chart, standing as the progenitors of the whole mess, are names not of suprapersonal "movements" but of individual artists, Van Gogh, Gauguin, Cézanne, and Seurat. Morey's Rieglian developmental scheme is here merged with the far older art historiographical tradition of the heroic individual artist, a tradition associated with the Renaissance formulation of Giorgio Vasari and still practiced in countless monographic studies of major artists to the present day.[14]

In the field of art from the Renaissance to the present such schematic conceptions as Barr's can function as shorthand aides-mémoires without seriously threatening the notion that the production of and the original creative component of art might at least in some measure be related to the actions of artists. The early Middle Ages has not been so lucky, nor treated with such sympathy, and serious scholars can still attribute to the early medieval artist little significant creative force. One can indeed read extensively in some, certainly not all, recent scholarly literature treating early medieval art and find that the possibility of a substantial personal role played by the artist, or even by the patron, is not even considered; it is as if the artists of the period belonged to a different species. Of course no one would today produce a Moreyan chart, nor I hope and trust would anyone today teach such a schema to innocent students. Yet a subsequent and far more subtle approach has substituted the role of particular models for the grand neo-Hegelian forces of Riegl's *Kunstwollen,* particular models which can far better account for the evident diversity of early medieval art, while still allowing only a slight role to the creative original artist.

The methodological Bible of the model-seeking approach to early medieval art is Kurt Weitzmann's *Illustrations in Roll and Codex,* first published in 1947.[15] In his magisterial and still fundamental work Weitzmann lays out evidence for the importance of considering the transmission of pictorial ideas from one work of art, the model or prototype, to another, the copy, proposing an essentially philological method of recensional analysis. Weitzmann, by deliberate analogy with textual criticism, calls this approach picture criticism. The student of early medieval art should not then look at a single work in isolation, but should regard it as part of a family of related works, whose relationships can and should be summarized in a schematic geneaological stemma. For example, such a stemma was proposed for the illustrated Byzantine manuscripts of the liturgical homilies of Gregory of Nazianzenus by Weitzmann's student George Galavaris, in his 1969 contribution to the same series in which *Roll and Codex* appeared. There A and Y represent two "archetypal" illustrative cycles of the ninth century that can be reconstructed from their subsequent copies, as a text critic attempts to reconstruct the author's original words from later manuscripts (fig.3).[16] It may be noted in passing that of the nineteen manuscripts listed by Galavaris, only three are claimed as direct copies of surviving prototypes, while sixteen are claimed to be directly based upon the two lost "archetypes." Few stemmata for literary texts look like this!

In a powerful passage forming the conclusion of *Roll and Codex,* Weitzmann turns to the possible ramifications of this subtler form of schematic and genealogical analysis upon the description and assessment of the style of the individual artist, and finds that "the power of tradition may be so strong that the style of the models remains distinguishable or may even dominate the personal style of the copyist."[17] To illustrate this point he cites the stylistic differences ascertainable in the late tenth- or early eleventh-century Menologion of Basil II, a magnificent imperial manuscript highly unusual in that the eight different painters who illustrated the manuscript signed their names beside the miniatures that they had executed. On a single plate in *Roll and Codex* (fig.4) Weitzmann illustrates six miniatures from that book, arguing quite persuasively that fig.196 is most similar in style to fig.199, fig.197 to 200 and fig.198 to 201. In other words, stylistic links exist on the vertical axis of the plate, but in fact individual artistic personality exists on the horizontal axis, for figs.196-198 are all the signed work of Pantoleon, and figs.199-201 the signed work of Georgios.

According to Weitzmann, the explanation for this situation in the Basil Menologion is to be found in the style of the respective sources employed. Figs.196 and 199 represent images of saints, and are probably based upon an earlier illustrated menologion, a hagiographical compendium. Figs.197 and 200, with their more active poses and small jutting heads, are New Testament figures probably based upon an earlier illustrated Gospel lectionary. The more substantial and elegantly classicizing prophets in figs.198 and 201 are probably based upon an earlier illustrated prophet book. Weitzmann concludes in the last paragraph of his book that in medieval art "the style of the model as well as the style of the period in which the copyist works are preponderant and more conspicuous than the comparatively slight oscillations within the limited realm of personal expression."[18] I myself find Weitzmann's analysis of this particular work of art persuasive in its broad outlines, although it may be pointed out that he himself in his later addendum to the passage for the second printing of the book is willing to grant that individual style is present here, albeit overshadowed by the style of the model.[19] Yet is this really a "typical" case from which we can safely form a general picture of the early medieval artist's personal contribution to his own work? It would be perverse to deny the importance of models in the creation of medieval works of art, and Weitzmann and many others have certainly demonstrated the value of this approach in many studies, yet most scholars would, I believe, take the Basil Menologion as an extreme, not a typical case. In light of the long tradition of attributing scant originality to early medieval artists, the following remarks seek to redress the balance by sketching some examples from the other end of the spectrum, in which models were of relatively minor importance or absent altogether, while recognizing that the great majority of cases likely fall somewhere in between.

Originality, Self-esteem and Self-consciousness

Early medieval artists or patrons did not establish the individual artist's originality as the central criterion of value in a work of art, as it would become in the modern period, or at least in the historiography of the modern period. A major problem in the discussion of early medieval artistic originality is in fact the profound difference between contemporary and early medieval literary sources, upon which scholars have inevitably drawn for an articulate presentation of early medieval writers' own self-perceptions, and which appear to provide relatively scant evidence for a view of originality as an important factor. There is certainly no medieval Michelangelo writing verse and letters in which his attitude toward artistic activity is revealed, no medieval Vasari reporting upon the great artists of the period and their creative genius.[20] The only early medieval artistic *vita* that I can cite, that of the seventh-century Frankish goldsmith Eligius of Noyon,[21] is a life of St. Eloi as a religious figure, not a life of Eloi the moneyer and artist, an activity very much beside the author's main point.[22] Many of our most important sources for early medieval works of art are indeed to be found in the *vitae* of saints, such as Bede's well-known lives of the abbots of Monkwearmouth and Jarrow and Stephanus' life of Wilfrid of Hexham.[23] However, the fact that the descriptions of buildings and paintings and books in those *vitae* say nothing about the original achievement of the artists who made them ought to be understood not as a lack of appreciation or regard for that achievement by the author, much less by the artists themselves, but rather as a consequence of the artistic descriptions' function as witness to the achievement of the holy patron, the focus of the literary genre.

If our literary sources by their very character fail to provide evidence that individual early medieval artists regarded themselves and were regarded by their contemporaries as creative artists with "independently determining imagination," to what evidence can we turn? In spite of the commonly held view that medieval artists labored in deliberate and pious anonymity, a view that Peter Cornelius Claussen not long ago labelled as a "romantische Fiktion" which nonetheless "munter fortblüht," we do in fact have a substantial number of artists' names and signatures, even from the early Middle Ages.[24] The Basil Menologion cited earlier is at least in this respect not an isolated case, especially in regard to the early medieval art of the Latin west. For example, the magnificent seventh-century fibula from Wittislingen, now in Munich (figs.5 and 6), is inscribed on its back with the name of its maker

Wigerig,[25] and we know the names of other fine metalworkers from literary sources.[26] Wigerig's signature is particularly interesting on two different levels. First, it occurs in conjunction with an apotropaic invocation on behalf of the patron. Apparently Wigerig sought some association with the supernatural potency of an object that he had himself brought into existence, and thus links himself with the ancient tradition of the smith as a powerful conjurer which may be found as a theme in both the art and literature of the early Middle Ages.[27] Second, it is difficult to escape the conclusion that one purpose of Wigerig in using his own name on the fibula was simply pride, and even what we might anachronistically term advertising; the brooch is no typical fibula, but of particularly magnificent materials and workmanship, and also embodies the most up-to-date international fashion in so-called Style II metalwork.[28] Names of artists, as in this case, commonly accompany exceptional works, not ordinary works, and presumably the greater prevalence of signatures in the very finest material signifies some awareness of distinctively high achievement on the part of the artists. Many of them, incidentally, enjoyed quite high social status, an important collateral issue which space prevents me from addressing here.[29]

Names of artists are especially common in the field of manuscript illumination, where the tradition of the scribal colophon allows us to refer to scribes of famous and luxuriously illustrated books such as Godescalc, Gundohinus, Cutbercht, MacRegol, Dagulf, Liuthard, Theodore and many others. Many of these colophons go far beyond mere signatures and repetitive formulae to attest the high esteem in which the scribe held his own work and apparently expected it to be held by the lucky recipient. For example, in the elaborately decorated colophon of his Lectionary presented to Charlemagne between 781-783 (fig.7), the scribe and artist Godescalc claims a high symbolic and even anagogical function for his decorative work:

> Golden letters on purple pages promise the heavenly kingdoms and the joys of heaven by the shedding of rosy blood. Divine precepts decorated with the color of roses demonstrate that the gifts of the martyrs should be accepted.... So the doctrine of God, written in precious metals, leads those following the light of the Gospels with a pure heart into the shining halls of the kingdom flowing with light, and sets those who climb above the high stars of heaven's vault in the bridal chamber of the king of heaven forever.

As David Ganz noted in his discussion of the passage, "such verses are without precedent."[30] The evident literary originality and sense of great accomplishment surely conveys something of the artist's sense of his own creative and novel visual achievement in producing what is still, in spite of heroic attempts to attach it to an earlier artistic tradition,[31] a startling departure from preceding works not only in its script and rich ornamental treatment of every page of text, but also in its extraordinary images of Christ and the evangelists (fig.8).[32]

Another manuscript written for Charlemagne about twelve years later finds its scribe Dagulf writing a poem about his book, giving that poem its own full page and echoing Godescalc's sentiments with the statement that "Golden words resound. Behold the golden letters paint David's psalms. Songs like these should be ornamented so well. They promise golden kingdoms and a lasting good without end."[33] Clearly, however, Dagulf is not simply copying Godescalc, who was probably personally known to him since both call themselves *famuli* of the king, that is members of the royal household, but is seeking to rival and surpass him. Examples of pictorial echoes may be not just the products of a conservative and unoriginal milieu but quite the reverse, highly conscious exchanges or even contests in which one individual seeks to outdo another, as has now been convincingly shown in the contemporary "imitative" poetry of the court figures such as Alcuin and Theodulf, by Peter Godman, Dieter Schaller and others.[34] Such personal rivalries evidently encouraged self-assertion and a desire for novel effects, while at the same time betokening a recognition of unusually creative achievements on the part of the contemporary audience.[35]

By the tenth century we have not only colophons but visual self-portraits by the scribe-illuminators,[36] as for example Keraldus and Heribertus presenting their work to Archbishop Egbert of Trier in a book written before 993. To be sure, the scale and posture of the artists are unmistakably subservient to the enormous patron enthroned between them, but their presence with him and the presence of their names and that of their monastery of Reichenau surely recognizes their justifiable pride in creating a work which in style and iconography represents a sharp departure from earlier patterns of illumination and helped establish a tradition followed by scores of later manuscripts for a period of many decades.[37] A less well-known Spanish example from the late tenth century presents the scribe on the same page and on the same scale with contemporary Leonese and earlier Visigothic kings.[38] Such self-portraits are not as assertive and self-congratulatory as the mid-twelfth-century image of the monastic scribe-painter Eadwine of Canterbury (fig.9), who prefaced his Psalter, which is in fact a direct, albeit much altered, copy of the famous Carolingian book in Utrecht, with an independent self-portrait bearing the inscription, "I am the prince of writers; neither my fame nor my praise will die quickly."[39] Yet the undeniable contrast between the images and the sentiments they embody should not be overdrawn, nor the apparent humility of the Reichenau monks' pose taken too literally. We should be warned by Charles Dickens' unforgettable character Uriah Heep that frequent and even abject professions of humility can in fact assert great pride, and should

remember that in the scribal colophon humility is a topos, a nearly universal fixture of the literary genre.[40] Even Eadwine in his self-portrait goes on
to say that "the worthiness of this book demonstrates your excellence, O
God."[41] Any good Christian reader of St. Augustine must know that all
virtue comes as a divine gift,[42] and that to attribute such virtue or skill
to oneself is a serious sin.[43] Such sentiments no more signify a lack of self-
regard in art than Benedictine discipline and asceticism indicate anything of
the sort in contemporary monastic life, and monastic writers from Benedict
onwards make abundantly clear the monk's essential concern with his own
personal salvation.[44] Indeed, drawing in part upon this very monastic conception, early medieval rulers on several occasions were shown in positions
of humility as a means of asserting their worthiness to rule, so that humility
becomes in fact a means of exaltation.[45]

The early medieval artist Valerianus may have intended, as Heinrich
Klotz suggested, to literally illustrate the Pauline concept that one should
not "glory save in the cross of our Lord Jesus Christ" (Gal. 6.14) by writing his own name at the center of a large jeweled cross surrounded by his
extensive scribal colophon (fig.10).[46] I am inclined to doubt that so specific
an evocation of that particular text was intended, but he certainly accomplished in fact a self-glorification with and through Christ, achieved through
what seems an entirely original artistic image with no known precedent or
successor. Images of the cross are to be sure often associated with colophons,
signatures and even scribal self-portraits, and images of artists and especially
of donors at the foot of the cross are very common,[47] but I know of no other
instance in which the scribe wraps himself in the mantle of the cross. That
Valerianus in his image expresses both humility and pride in his achievement,
indeed expresses pride through his humility, is an interpretation lent support
by other aspects of his Gospelbook, since Valerianus elsewhere several times
indulges in some Greek lettering which is a rather common form of scribal
showboating.[48]

The nature of Christianity as a religion of the book, and the identification
of Christ himself as the Word, inevitably gave great prestige and importance
to the work of those who transcribed Holy Scripture. The extraordinarily
luxurious decoration with which an entire class of early medieval Gospelbooks
was endowed bears direct and eloquent witness to the enormous prestige and
value connected with such works. Not only did the scribes of sacred volumes
step into the position of the smiths, as makers of objects with supernatural potency,[49] they also took over the position of the evangelists themselves,
who in the early medieval western tradition are commonly depicted not as
authors displaying their works but as scribes physically engaged in putting
words on parchment with the tools still used by the laborers in contemporary
scriptoria. For example, the first canon table from a manuscript preserved at

Flavigny and probably written in central France in the later eighth century, now Autun, Bibliothèque Municipale MS 4, fol. 8r (fig.11), shows all four evangelists with pens and other writing implements. At the same time, two of the four evangelists distinctly look upward at their "symbols" gathered around Christ, from whom they stem and whose good news they reveal by inspiring the writers on earth below.[50] The evangelists are presented as divinely inspired scribes, and in many other portrait miniatures they appear as if seized by the sort of divine frenzy identified as the very essence of the Neoplatonic idea of creative genius associated with a Renaissance conception of artistic originality.[51] That the notion of angelically-transmitted inspiration remains a fixture of modern views of creativity is shown by a recent drawing by Jack Ziegler, whose humor and idea derive from that Renaissance conception, but whose form stems directly from medieval evangelist portraits (fig.12).[52]

Surely the artists who produced the very numerous evangelist portraits in early medieval manuscripts can be shown to have drawn upon, even if they virtually never closely replicated, earlier versions of their subject, but at that same time their production of images of their predecessors in the writing of Holy Scripture must have influenced their attitude toward the value of their own creative activity. Such an attitude need not be merely inferred. The form of the scribe's self-portrait in the Eadwine Psalter (fig.9) is only one of many examples whose form is manifestly derived from an evangelist portrait. We also have the eloquent witness to the high status of the scribe's craft from a ninth-century monastic author intimately familiar with the manufacture of luxurious and novel books, Hrabanus Maurus of Fulda:

> Lex pia cumque dei latum dominans regit orbem,
>   Quam sanctum est legem scribere namque dei!
> Est pius ille labor, merito cui non valet alter
>   Aequiparare, manus quem faciet hominis.
> Nam digiti scripto laetantur, lumina visu,
>   Mens volvet sensu mystica verba dei.

> (As God's kindly law rules in absolute majesty over the wide world, it is an exceedingly holy task to copy the law of God. This activity is a pious one, unequalled in merit by any other which men's hands can perform. For the fingers rejoice in writing, the eyes in seeing, and the mind at examining the meaning of God's mystical words.)[53]

Hrabanus himself was responsible for an extraordinary quasi-self- portrait image in the last of the extraordinary series of twenty-eight acrostic picture-poems that constitute his *De laudibus sanctae crucis*, written in 810 (fig.13). It depicts him as a monk kneeling at the foot of the cross, and continues the theme of colophon images and texts already discussed, with the letters contained within his body spelling the prayer, "Rabanum memet clemens rogo Criste tuere o pie iudicio" ("I beseech you, O merciful Christ, benevolently to protect me, Hrabanus, in the Judgment").[54]

It is not very likely that literary sources will provide much additional insight concerning the early medieval artists' attitude toward creative originality. The sources have been extensively mined for a long time,[55] and it is not to be expected that some early medieval equivalent of Michelangelo's sonnets lurks undiscovered in them. *Pingere* and *scribere*, "to paint" and "to write" in classical Latin, in fact function as virtual synonyms throughout the early Middle Ages, and either word can be used for either activity. The Anglo-Saxon colophon of the great Lindisfarne Gospels says that Eadfrith merely "wrote" the book, although few now or then would deny that the manuscript was magnificently "painted."[56] The unavoidable problem that early medieval Latin, and for that matter Greek,[57] lacks any clear and consistent jargon describing artistic activity manifestly does not prove that the activity did not in fact exist, and indeed we see it staring us in the face in numerous surviving works of art. The plain fact is that in searching for the originality of the early medieval artist we need to look not at rare and highly problematic texts, but at very abundant and often quite wonderful works of art.

Originality and Creativity

I hope that the preceding discussion has helped to clarify the historiographical background for the notion that early medieval artists were not original, has indicated that the anonymity and humility of the early medieval artist has been much overstated, and has shown evidence that early medieval artists did in fact have high regard for their own work, a regard shared by other members of their society. Self-esteem and recognition of social status are not, however, identical with originality as that term is normally used by art historians. Indeed, artists who were lions of the Salon, extravagantly praised and rewarded in their own day, may now be found lacking in originality, and it is a hackneyed central myth of modern art and art history that the truly original geniuses, the wellsprings of creativity, were likely to be spurned in their own day.[58] Yet post-modernist criticism of the excessive claims made for itself by the avant-garde should not prevent us from presenting a moderate case for the possible originality of at least some early medieval artists.

Creativity remains the central element of originality. In one sense, it seems self-evident that medieval artists were creative, that the great number of superlative works of such extraordinary diversity obviously stems from more than a series of mistakes. Nonetheless it may be useful to consider a few selected examples of early medieval works in terms of five artificially

separated categories, that is, formal or stylistic arrangements, technical procedures, expression, subject matter, and function. Within each of these five
categories we should consider three questions, the degree of novelty with
respect to what may be termed either a living tradition or a particular prototype or model, the degree to which any perceived novelty appears to stem
from deliberate action as opposed to mistakes, misunderstandings, deficiencies, or the inevitable workings of training and other such factors, and finally
and most difficult, whether any residual deliberate novelty found to exist constituted a valued and significant aspect of the work of art in the opinion of its
maker and/or its audience. I think we can probably all agree that a work of
art novel in respect to any precedents, deliberately rather than accidentally
novel, and whose novelty is considered a criterion of positive worth ought to
be found guilty of originality.

First, it must be readily admitted that the simple fact of ascertainable
artistic individuality does not in and of itself constitute what we are seeking
to assess as originality. All art historical scholars practice "connoisseurship"
in some sense, and the fact that we can distinguish seven distinct scribal
hands even in so rigidly controlled a manuscript as the late seventh-century
Codex Amiatinus from Northumbria does not really make any of the scribes
very "original" in their script, since all are carefully copying a particular early
Italian model.[59] Such differences as can be recognized by modern scholars
among the Wearmouth-Jarrow scribes, minute in this case, much greater
in others, are the irreducible traces of different hands, Kessler's "personal
traits." These differences are no more signs of what we mean by originality
in the early Middle Ages than they are in modern European painting, the field
where modern connoisseurship was created, and where followers of Giovanni
Morelli can distinguish one minor and largely derivative artist's work from
another's by carefully observing the configuration of earlobes.[60] To find the
conscious and significant originality of the early medieval artist it is necessary
to go beyond mere individuality.

Let me begin with the critical issue of style.[61] The reason for my definition of style as critical ought already to be clear from the preceding discussion. Because of the long emphasis upon the history of visual style as the
central core of art history, as in many respects the essential and uniquely
art historical problem, in the works of Riegl, Wölfflin and many others, the
question of the original individual contribution to works of art has focused
on notions of style and form. However, even when we look at the development of the so-called barbarian metalworking styles of the fifth and sixth
centuries in northwestern Europe, the kind of material that Riegl used to
develop and test his ideas, recent research has found the Rieglian notion of
an immanent artistic development or *Kunstwollen* an inadequate explanation
of diversity and change.[62] Thus the polychrome style of gold cells containing

geometrically cut garnet stones "develops" very little between a late fifth-century work like the sword fittings from the tomb of Childeric at Tournai and the mid-seventh-century fragment of the great cross made by St. Eloi of Noyon for St. Denis, while in other ornamental styles the change of style during the same period is quite rapid. Similarly, essentially the same style is practiced by the late fifth-century and early sixth-century metalworkers in Frankish and in Italian territory, as in the great eagle fibula and other Ostrogothic jewelry from Domagnano (fig.14).[63] The style is both stable and international at the highest level of production and patronage, it is a court style in other words,[64] with aulic associations that encourage a certain conservatism, and it seems therefore that it was deliberately adopted in a wide variety of contexts because of its associations. On the other hand the late sixth and early seventh-century ribbon-interlace style known to archaeologists since Bernhard Salin as "Style II"[65] was international in distribution, but not nearly so stable or long-lived as the polychrome style. Style II jewelry suddenly appears in the last quarter of the sixth century in Anglo-Saxon England, in Scandinavia, across the Frankish territories and into Germany, and in Lombard Italy, and for a long time archaeologists debated the question of where the style originated. It was clearly not a gradual development of a previous ornamental style à la Riegl, but a new invention, now generally thought to have been the product of a Lombard craftsman who sought to combine Germanic animal styles with Mediterranean interlace ornament.[66] The style clearly owed its very rapid dissemination to what might best be called "fashion," spread into other media such as book illumination, and certainly implies a clear attraction to variety and novelty on the part of both artists and patrons. Hence it is characteristic of Style II to be very commonly combined with other techniques so as to display the artist's craft and evidently his originality, as again on the Wittislingen brooch previously cited in another context (fig.5), where Style II animal forms and interlace are combined with elements of the polychrome style in an unusual manner. Although Style II ornament could be and was commonly used, like the polychrome style, in royal contexts, it was just as clearly not limited to such contexts, but quickly appeared in personal ornaments at all levels of society, not only in precious but also in base materials. Far from being indicative of a suprapersonal stylistic development, such metalwork cannot be understood at all without recognizing the variety of conscious decisions and the pursuit of novel effects by artists and patrons alike.

To be sure, early medieval artists could and not infrequently did make copies as accurately as they could do so. Perhaps the most famous example is provided by the Codex Amiatinus, the great Northumbrian Bible of the late seventh century already mentioned in relation to its highly disciplined scribes. Its introductory decorated pages with a large picture of the Old

Testament Tabernacle and digrammatic tables of contents according to the systems of Augustine, Hilary and Jerome were copied so accurately from the illustrations in an Italian Bible described by the sixth-century Italian author Cassiodorus that for a long time scholars thought these illustrations had been simply lifted bodily from a Cassiodoran Bible. The same was said of the richly painted and apparently classicizing portrait of the scribe Ezra in his study (fig.15), with its complex volumetric shading of forms and use of cast shadows. Even after Rupert Bruce-Mitford provided abundant and to most scholars persuasive evidence to show that the painter was a seventh-century Anglo-Saxon monk,[67] some have been reluctant to grant this possibility,[68] perhaps in part because if it is true that early medieval artists could make such extremely accurate copies when they wished to do so, then it is very difficult to understand the great diversity of early medieval artistic works without accepting the proposition that as a general rule early medieval artists did not wish to copy their models as accurately as possible.

Mere shuffling among different models and recombining details from different sources by uncreative copyists simply cannot explain the artistic material that survives. For example, the portrait of the evangelist Matthew in the slightly later Northumbrian Lindisfarne Gospels (fig.16) derives its seated figure of the evangelist either from the Codex Amiatinus itself or from that manuscript's earlier Italian model, but combines the figure with the winged symbol of the evangelist above his head drawn from an entirely different source, probably the frame from another model, and the peculiar figure peering from behind a curtain from a fourth source, or indeed the artist invented the motif on his own initiative.[69] Yet the style of the miniature as a whole is completely consistent and unified. Although the basic posture of the seated figure in the model is very closely followed by the Lindisfarne artist, who even improves upon the drawing of the hands and feet in terms of their naturalism, that artist completely transforms the technique and style of the figure, for example rejecting the classical mixing of different tones within each hue in favor of a much brighter palette of pure hues only. In other words we see two nearly contemporary monastic artists from Northumbria looking at the same model, one producing a nearly perfect copy, and the other transforming the prototype. Nothing very much like the Lindisfarne miniature itself provided a direct model for the Lindisfarne miniature as a whole, and the artist was clearly aware of the radical transformation that he was effecting. In these senses his work obviously deserves to be credited with originality. The simple fact that the artist is taking an earlier work as a point of departure by no means in and of itself entails a lack of originality. Indeed, a number of years ago Hanns Swarzenski used the relationship between these two works as one instance of what he termed "creative copying," a phenomenon which he saw as critical and commonplace not only in the early medieval period but throughout later western art into the twentieth century.[70] We have no explicit evidence that in making this novel transformation the Lindisfarne artist thought that he was creating a superior work, but I find it very hard to believe that such was not the case in this instance.

Of technique there is a great deal that might be said concerning the originality of early medieval artists. Excellence in craftsmanship is a critical term of praise in descriptions of works of art from the period. All artists learn their craft from a teacher up to a certain level, and in their mature work can adopt other techniques of which they become aware in a variety of possible ways, so that technique is always likely to be more a result of tradition that originality. However, during the early medieval period there is abundant evidence that artists were willing and indeed interested in exploring the unknown, in doing new things and doing old things in new ways. In his famous description of Justinian's new Hagia Sophia, Procopius stresses the novelty of such features as the suspended "pressed together triangles" beneath the dome,[71] since pendentives had never before been used to support a large dome, and no reader of this wonderful description can doubt that what Richard Krautheimer has called the "shockingly bold interior" of the church was seen as an original achievement of great beauty and rich meaning.[72] Another architectural work provides additional evidence of the invention and appreciation of new techniques, albeit in a different sense. Recently Eugene Kleinbauer argued that the famous Plan of St. Gall (fig.23), drawn around 820, represents "the first time in Western or Eastern Mediterranean art, [not only from the medieval but also from the ancient world, that] a drawing played a large role in conveying one individual's architectural concepts to someone else."[73] He sees the use of a consistent scale as another novel feature of the drawing, and terms the plan "one of a number of Carolingian works of significant originality, without known precedent."[74]

In the visual arts, the recent discovery of a collection of important eighth and early ninth-century fabrics in the church of St. Catherine at Maaseik sheds new light on innovative early medieval techniques of textile manufacture. The material includes the earliest known example of the laid and couched work later to gain fame as *opus anglicanum,* a means of embroidery invented by early medieval English women, as it would seem. The same collection also provides astonishing evidence that by the ninth century woven silk fabrics were already being produced in the west, as witnessed by the repeat pattern of an enthroned figure in a medallion labelled David in Latin letters of distinctively Anglo-Saxon character.[75] Metalworkers of the period combined different techniques in unprecedented ways, and created new variants of older procedures. The great goldsmith of the Sutton Hoo burial is perhaps the outstanding example of technical innovation, and of sheer splendor of craftsmanship.[76] His tiny pyramidal sword mounts continue the gold-and-garnet technique of the polychrome style, appropriate in this royal context, but he combines the traditional cloisonné technique with millefiori enamelwork for the little central checkerboard, while also exposing some garnets at the corners so that they must be cut on three different surfaces at difficult oblique angles. Both features are unprecedented, and the latter especially clearly indicates a deliberate tour-de-force display. For the great hinged shoulderclasps, which, characteristically and revealingly, differ from one another in subtle ways, the same goldsmith, whose personal style and approach is easily recognizable even though we do not know his name, used two unprecedented technical procedures (fig.17). He cut his garnets not only into small geometric shapes, but also into large plates that could take large and complex zoomorphic shapes, as here a single stone forms the hind leg of each of the affronted and interwoven wild boars. He also made a thin gold lid to cover some of his cells so as to give the effect of a solid gold background against which his figural subject could stand out more clearly.[77] Both procedures are novel, deliberate in contributing to an enlargement and clarification of the complex late Style II animal ornament, and positively radiate the artist's pride in his splendidly successful original creations.

In the sphere of new expression it would be easy to cite many examples in Carolingian art alone which embody a fundamentally novel and deliberate evocation of emotional and psychological intensity. One immediately thinks of the wonderfully expressive figures of the Utrecht Psalter, or of Anglo-Saxon drawings stemming from the same tradition of rapid linear draughtsmanship. Even if certain aspects of this style owe something to an earlier model or models, as has frequently been suggested, it seems to me impossible to deny the freshness and impact of such works.[78] Indeed, in a recent article which takes the general derivation from an earlier model for granted, and emphasizes the strong impact of the "common schooling practiced at Reims," Joachim Gaehde nevertheless stressed the artists' "considerable stylistic freedom vis-à-vis their models," with the "briskly linear modes and expressive force owned by masters C and F [being] free translations."[79]

In the present context I would like only to look at a single Ottonian ivory, now in Berlin, produced at Echternach in the second quarter of the eleventh century, and illustrating the Incredulity of Thomas (fig.18).[80] The contrast between its tensely compacted composition and the elegant symmetry and reserved dignity of a nearly contemporary Byzantine version of the same event, whether in a miniature or in another ivory such as the panel from Dumbarton Oaks (fig.19), is obviously very great.[81] The Byzantine composition ultimately stems from late Roman imperial iconography, but is at the same time in some respects more accurate in terms of the description of the event in John 20.26-7:

> And after eight days again his disciples were within, and Thomas with them. Jesus cometh, the doors being shut, and stood in the midst, and said: Peace be to you. Then saith he to Thomas: Put in thy finger hither, and see my hands; and bring hither thy hand, and put it into my side; and be not faithless, but believing.

The Byzantine ivory shows all twelve disciples, with Christ in their midst, as called for by the text, but the Ottonian artist eliminates the witnesses to leave only the central actors in the drama. The Byzantine ivory shows the closed doors and implies the interior setting specified by the text, but the Ottonian artist eliminates these details. On the other hand, where the Byzantine artist shrinks back from showing the climactic moment, when Thomas places his hand in Christ's wound, this is precisely what the Ottonian artist emphasizes. At the same time he turns Thomas' back to the viewer, who literally looks over Thomas' shoulder and is drawn into the space in a far more intimate and personal way. The serpentine disjointed body of Thomas, and the way his head is hunched down into his shoulders perhaps suggests his shame and sin in not being willing to believe without physical proof; Jesus says, "Because thou hast seen me, Thomas, thou hast believed: blessed are they that have not seen, and have believed." The viewer's faith is addressed and challenged in a direct and powerful way through this work, whose composition is distinct not only from possible Byzantine prototypes, but from earlier Ottonian compositions, such as the ivory from Magdeburg, which emphasizes the narrative elements of the interior setting, the closed door, and the witnessing college of apostles.[82]

When we turn to the realm of subject matter it is immediately clear that medieval artists invented a host of new images, and by this I do not mean simply illustrations for new events that perforce required some manner of invention such as the conquest of England depicted in the Bayeux Tapestry or the lives of recent saints such as Cuthbert, depicted in several manuscript cycles. Rather I mean also new interpretations of images having long traditions. The scene of the Crucifixion of Christ furnishes a good example. Prior to the early Middle Ages Christ was always shown alive on the cross, with eyes open, but by the ninth and tenth centuries the subject of the dead Christ on the cross begins to appear frequently in both Byzantine and western works of art.[83] Here it is also clear that the new motif is used for expressive purposes, as well as to convey important theological doctrines emphasizing Christ's full humanity. Shortly after the theme of the dead Christ begins to be shown, he is also portrayed with a crown which is both a martyr's and particularly a royal crown, as in a late tenth or eleventh-century Ottonian ivory (fig.20),[84] an important motif emphasizing Christ's full divinity and heralding the later medieval Christomimetic conception of the royal office. Such important shifts in subject matter cannot have been effected entirely or even primarily by the originality of individual artists, however, and reflect the changing demands of patrons and perceptions of audiences. The same may very likely be true for many of the other new subjects, but certainly not for all. Who invented the famous unique composition in the late tenth-century Reichenau Gospels of Otto III, depicting Otto in heavenly majesty, borne aloft by earth and flanked by the symbols of the evangelists (fig.21)? Clearly it is an invention, whose precedents are all images of Christ enthroned, not of any secular ruler, and the invention was evidently deemed so unorthodox that it was not followed by later artists, even if its ideas can be found expressed in a less provocative manner in a variety of other innovative regalian images of the period.[85] It is unlikely that the emperor himself suggested the iconography, and although the ecclesiastical patron is a more likely candidate, we know from the previously cited dedication portrait of the Reichenau monks Keraldus and Heribertus presenting their book to Archbishop Egbert of Trier that Reichenau artists produced luxurious books for quite remote patrons, and presumably worked with a considerable degree of independence. Although patrons may have suggested programs and ideas, they expected artists to be able to execute the artistic details of their commissions in a creative way.

In a number of other works of art with new subject matter there is almost no possibility of doubting that the artist was personally and very self-consciously responsible for the novelty. The example that always comes first to my mind in this regard is the miniature of the tetramorph in the Gospels now in the Trier Cathedral treasury, MS 61, probably written at the monastery of Echternach in or about the 720's (fig.22).[86] Here all four evangelist symbols are combined to make a single figure with human torso atop the legs of a man, of a lion, of a bull, and the wings of an eagle. There are precedents for devoting a miniature to the four evangelists' symbols, to be sure. The four creatures surround a cross in the earlier Book of Durrow,[87] as well as in a number of other books, and there can be no doubt that the Trier 61 artist knew such a composition, since he copied something of this sort elsewhere in his book.[88] Some earlier images of theophanies roll the four creatures into a sort of single creature, as for example in the tetramorph bearing the chariot in the Ascension miniature of the sixth-century Syriac Rabbula Gospels,[89] and the Trier 61 artist may also have known something of this sort. Yet the specific form of the tetramorph in the Trier Gospels, and its appearance as the central subject of a separate miniature, are unprecedented. That the artist knew he was making something new here and was proud of doing so is evident from his choice of this page for his signature, visible at the bottom of the image: *Thomas scribsit,* or Thomas wrote this.[90]

That the early medieval artist could develop new functions for and with works of art is evident from the Plan of St. Gall already mentioned for its innovative technique (fig.23).[91] The large transepted basilica at the heart of the plan is derived directly or indirectly from the prototype of the apostolic basilicas of St. Peter's and St. Paul's in Rome, and the annular crypt passage surely reflects the same source. As Walter Horn has argued, for me persuasively, the design of the various subsidiary buildings such as the house for distinguished visitors seems to directly stem from the traditions of northern timber architecture, with its essential skeletal system of construction. On the other hand, there can be no doubt that the plan as a whole is shockingly novel and original, as is especially the case for the planning of the cloister area, with the essential spaces of dormitory and refectory grouped around a courtyard in which the monks could have access to light and air while remaining strictly segregated from the outside world, "cloistered" in other words. The plan represents an intelligent and original solution to the new problem posed by large and wealthy monasteries which performed important economic, political and intellectual functions while attempting to preserve their essential spiritual identity and purpose.

The Plan of St. Gall is a "machine for monastic living," and its enormous success is attested by the hundreds of later western monasteries that follow the broad outlines of the plan. It is important to note, however, that none copy it exactly, and this fact cannot in my view be due simply to the differences of terrain, mistakes and the like. Although I myself doubt Horn's hypothesis that the plan was drawn up by a sort of building subcommittee of the great Carolingian monastic reform conferences held at Aachen in 816 and 817, and believe that the plan was designed by Bishop Haito of Basel in a manner that reflects at least some of the spirit of the conference's reforms, there is no room for doubt as to how the plan was supposed to be used by its recipient, Abbot Gozbert of St. Gall. The original dedicatory inscription survives at the top of the sheet, and although the interpretation of the text in detail remains the subject of lively scholarly debate, for the present purpose there is no need to quarrel with Horn's translation where Haito tells Gozbert that he is presenting him with "this briefly annotated copy of the layout of the monastic buildings, with which you may exercise your ingenuity."[92] Clearly Haito is proud of his very elaborate plan, but clearly also expects, as we would no doubt expect today in similar circumstances, that Gozbert will look at and no doubt learn from the monastic plan presented for his inspection, selecting what is useful and attractive to him while changing aspects that seem to him inappropriate or undesirable for his own community. The very process of looking at models is here conceived as an individual creative activity.

In the final analysis, it seems to me that no dialectical necessity forces us to choose between either copying or originality as the driving force in the work of the early medieval artist. Neither factor can be presumed to be by itself sufficient in any given instance, and research needs to seek and reveal the interaction between these and other factors such as the role of the patron and audience. Still it seems that the achievement of individual medieval artists has been undervalued in relationship to later western artists, whose works often owe as much to patronage and earlier pictorial models and traditions, as scholarship has demonstrated again and again. Few artistic masterpieces are better known than Gian Lorenzo Bernini's Cornaro Chapel in S. Maria della Vittoria in Rome, whose central motif depicts the ecstasy of S. Teresa as she is pierced by the arrow of divine love held by the angel above her (fig.24).[93] The motif of the piercing arrow is derived directly from the saint's own account of her vision, but that account itself inevitably reflects earlier mystical literature and mystical art. Of course, none of the "derivative" features diminish Bernini's achievement or our perception of its fundamental "originality." To me equally moving and "original" in every sense is the related conception and composition traditionally, if not conclusively, regarded as a self-portrait by the great Saxon monastic reformer St. Dunstan, which served as a frontispiece to the miscellany known as his classbook (fig.25).[94] The spear or arrow of righteousness and power held by the enormous looming figure of Christ descends toward the praying monk, while the inscribed tablet welcomes those whose fear of God will help them to learn. To understand this rich and complex image one needs to assess both the process of copying and adapting earlier sources and the addition of individual, meaningful alterations in that process. Medieval art historians have by now well learned to look for sources, and accordingly find them very often. I am convinced that if we look more thoroughly and sympathetically for the originality of the early medieval artist, we will find that very often as well.

Notes

I am grateful to Ernst Kitzinger and Horst Bredekamp for having read a preliminary draft of this paper, and for having offered valuable comments and bibliographical suggestions, although neither should be held culpable for remaining errors and infelicities of thought and expression. Robert Deshman, Jonathon Alexander and Elly Miller generously helped with the acquisition of necessary photographs.

1. Among earlier studies specifically addressed to the topic may be mentioned Jacques Guilmain, "The Forgotten Medieval Artist," *Art Journal* 25 (1965): 33-42.

2. Herbert Kessler, "On the State of Medieval Art History," *Art Bulletin* 70 (1988): 166-187, especially 179.

3. Herbert Kessler, "An Apostle in Armor and the Mission of Carolingian Art," *Arte medievale,* 2nd ser., 4 (1990): 17-41.

4. Kessler, "State," 182.

5. Jeffrey Anderson, "On the Nature of the Theodore Psalter," *Art Bulletin* 70 (1988): 550-568, especially 552-553.

6. Both formulations occupy common ground in stating that the intention of medieval artists can be narrowly and accurately defined. Such a belief that intentionality is largely recoverable is considered rather quaint and unsupportable by some recently popular critical stances, but is an old-fashioned view that I would be loath to give up altogether. Recognizing, as we ought to recognize, all the limitations of our contemporary perspective, and the impossibility of achieving a fully correct reconstruction of an artist's intention, it nonetheless seems to me an effort worth the making, and one from which scholars can learn, and have for a very long time in fact learned a good deal. In the context of the problem of artistic originality to be addressed here, the question of intent seems to me unavoidable however one chooses to define originality, and I do not believe that the question should be simply dismissed as undebatable merely because it is ultimately unanswerable. See now for the general problem of intentionality in art Michael Baxandall, *Patterns of Intention: On the Historical Explanation of Pictures* (New Haven, 1985), and the theoretical discussion by David Summers, "Intentions in the History of Art," *New Literary History* 17 (1986): 305-321, along with the response by Steven Z. Levine and Summers' reply on 323-332 and 333-344 respectively in the same journal issue.

7. *The Compact Edition of the Oxford English Dictionary* (Oxford, 1971), 1:2010.

8. See on this and related questions the stimulating essay by Hans Belting, *The End of the History of Art?*, trans. Christopher S. Wood (Chicago and London, 1987).

9. On the interesting problem posed by the term "masterpiece" in its development from medieval origins into the modern period see Walter Cahn, *Masterpieces: Chapters on the History of an Idea,* Princeton Essays on the Arts 7 (Princeton, 1979). I have borrowed the term "hero" from Sidney Hook, *The Hero in History. A Study in Limitation and Possibility* (Boston, 1943).

10. Alois Riegl, *Die spätrömische Kunst-industrie* (Vienna, 1901), trans. Rolf Winkes, *Late Roman Art Industry,* Archaeologica 36 (Rome, 1985). For a classic discussion of Riegl's concept see Erwin Panofsky, "Der Begriff des Kunstwollens," *Zeitschrift für Aesthetik und allgemeine Kunstwissenschaft* 14 (1926): 321-339, and for a more recent concise discussion of Riegl's work see Michael Podro, *The Critical Historians of Art* (New Haven and London, 1982), 71-97, with extensive bibliography.

11. The frequent criticism of the medieval tradition in nineteenth-century art historiography needs no demonstration, but it is also well to recognize that the criticism was by no means universal. The relationship between "abstract" medieval art and the new "abstract" modern art of the same period has recently begun to be explored, as for example in the very stimulating recent article by Madeline Caviness, "Broadening the Definitions of 'Art': the Reception of Medieval Works in the Context of Post-Impressionist Movements," in *Hermeneutics and Medieval Culture,* ed. Patrick J. Gallacher and Helen Damico (New York, 1989), 259-282.

12. Charles Rufus Morey, "The Sources of Medieval Style," *Art Bulletin* 7 (1924): 35-50. The geneaological chart stands at the conclusion of the article, on p. 50, and is introduced thus: "the significant cause of medieval style can be plotted with certainty and followed back to only two parent streams into which the Hellenistic divided."

13. Alfred Barr, *Cubism and Abstract Art* (New York, 1936). See for the development of this chart the stimulating discussion by Susan Platt Noyes, "Modernism, Formalism and Politics: the 'Cubism and Abstract Art' Exhibition of 1936 at the Museum of Modern Art," in "Revising Cubism," ed. Patricia Leighten, *Art Journal* 47 (1988): 284-295, especially 285-286 and figs.4 and 9.

14. See Hans Belting, "Vasari and his Legacy. The History of Art as a Process?" in his *End of the History of Art?,* 67-94.

15. Kurt Weitzmann, *Illustrations in Roll and Codex. A Study of the Origin and Method of Text Illustration,* Studies in Manuscript Illumination 2 (Princeton, 1947; new printing with addenda, 1970).

16. George Galavaris, *The Illustrations of the Liturgical Homilies of Gregory Nazianzanus*, Studies in Manuscript Illumination 6 (Princeton, 1969), 193. It is interesting to note that Weitzmann himself has seldom actually produced such a schema.

17. Weitzmann, *Roll and Codex*, 199.

18. Weitzmann, *Roll and Codex*, 205.

19. Weitzmann, *Roll and Codex* (1970 printing only), 260-261. He is here responding to the findings of Ihor Sevčenko, "The Illuminators of the Menologion of Basil II," *Dumbarton Oaks Papers* 16 (1962): 245-276.

20. For Michelangelo's writings see the convenient translation by Creighton Gilbert, *Complete Poems and Selected Letters of Michelangelo* (New York, 1965), and for a splendid discussion of the Renaissance artist's self-conception, Erwin Panofsky, "Artist, Scientist, Genius: Notes on the 'Renaissance-Dämmerung'," in Wallace K. Ferguson, et al., *The Renaissance* (New York, 1953), 121-182, especially 172-175 on the notion of the divine madness of artistic creation. See now however the powerful warning against the overestimation of Neoplatonism in the Renaissance by Horst Bredekamp, "Götterdämmerung des Neuplatonismus," *Kritische Berichte* 14 (1986): 39-48.

21. *Vita Eligii episcopi Noviomagensis*, in Bruno Krusch, ed., *Monumenta Germaniae Historica* (henceforth abbreviated as *MGH*), *Scriptorum rerum Merovingicarum* 4, *Passiones vitaeque sanctorum aevi Merovingici* (Hanover and Leipzig, 1902), 634-741.

22. For Eligius' artistic works see Hayo Vierck, "Werke des Eligius," in Georg Kossack and Günter Ulbert, eds., *Studien zur vor- und frühgeschichtlichen Archäologie. Festschrift für Joachim Werner zum 65. Geburtstag*, Münchner Beiträge zur Vor-und Frühgeschichte, Ergänzungsband 1 (Munich, 1974), 309-380. A particular emphasis upon the saint's artistic endeavors emerges in the early Renaissance environment, as in the famous portrait of the saint in his money-room painted by Petrus Christus in the mid-fifteenth century; see Peter Schabacker, *Petrus Christus* (Utrecht, 1974), 86-91 and fig.6.

23. For Bede see Christopher Plummer, ed., *Historia Abbatum*, in his *Baedae opera historica* (Oxford, 1896), trans. James Campbell, *Bede, The Ecclesiastical History of the English People and Other Selections* (New York, 1968), and for Wilfrid, Bertram Colgrave, ed. and trans., *The Life of Bishop Wilfrid by Eddius Stephanus* (Cambridge,1927).

24. Peter Cornelius Claussen, "Früher Künstlerstolz. Mittelalterliche Signaturen als Quelle der Kunstsoziologie," in Karl Clausberg, et al., eds., *Bauwerk und Bildwerk im Hochmittelalter. Anschauliche Beiträge zur Kultur- und Sozialgeschichte* (Giessen, 1981), 7-34. Claussen also makes the historiographical point that "die Wissenschaft von der Kunst ist selbst ein Kind

der Renaissance und für diese war der Triumph über das Mittelalter ein Teil des Selbstverständnisses und der Identitätsfindung. Diese polemische Erbteil hat die Kunstgeschichte niemals abgelegt." However, it should be noted that Claussen traces artistic signatures only as far back as the twelfth and early thirteenth centuries and then only in an Italian civic context, and in effect does not so much dissolve the medieval-Renaissance dichotomy in this regard as move the dawn of the Renaissance back a century or two.

25. See Rainier Christlein, *Die Alamannen: Archäologie eines lebendigen Volkes* (Stuttgart and Aalen, 1978), 101 and pls. 23 and 94.

26. For a convenient sample representing only Anglo-Saxon England during the period, see C.R. Dodwell, *Anglo-Saxon Art. A New Perspective* (Ithaca, 1982). From the index one culls the names of the following metalworkers, mostly known from literary sources: Aelfnoth, Aelfric, Aelfsige, Alward, Alwold, Billfrith, Biorhthelm, Brismet, Bryhtelm, Byrnelm, Cwicwine, Cytel, and so forth.

27. See Heinrich Beck, "Der kunstfertige Schmied - ein ikonographisches und narratives Thema des frühen Mittelalters," in Flemming G. Andersen, et al., eds., *Medieval Iconography and Narrative. A Symposium* (Odense, 1980), 15-37, with further literature.

28. See on the diffusion of this sharply novel artistic style, Günther Haseloff, "Der germanische Tierstil: seine Anfänge und der Beitrag der Langobarden," *Atti del convegno internazionale sul tema: La civiltà dei Langobardi in Europa*, Academia nazionale dei Lincei, Anno 371 (Rome, 1974), 361-386.

29. See on this issue the remarks by Dodwell, *Anglo-Saxon Art*, 44-83, and Karl Hauck, "Wielands Hort. Die sozialgeschichtliche Stellung des Schmiedes in frühen Bildprogrammen nach und vor dem Religionswechsel," *Antikvariskt Arkiv* 64 (1977): 5-31. The legal situation of artists appears to have been quite variable; for the legal status of artists in early medieval Ireland I look forward to the forthcoming study by Douglas MacLean. See also studies in three volumes edited by Xavier Barral i Altet, *Artistes, artisans et production artistique au moyen âge*, Colloque international, Centre National de la Recherche Scientifique, Université de Rennes II - Haute-Bretagne, 2-6 mai 1983 (Paris, 1986-1990).

30. David Ganz, "The Preconditions for Carolingian Minuscule," *Viator* 18 (1987): 23-43, especially 30. The translation is Ganz's own; for the Latin text see Ernst Dümmler, ed., *MGH, Poetarum latinorum medii aevi* 1, *Poetae latini aevi Carolini* (henceforth abbreviated as *PLAC*) 1 (Berlin, 1881), 94-95. Cf. the article in this volume by Thomas Noble, "From Brigandage to Justice," at nn.14 and 52.

31. Hans Belting, "Probleme der Kunstgeschichte Italiens im Frühmittelalter," *Frühmittelalterliche Studien* 1 (1967): 94-143.

32. For the manuscript and its decoration see Wilhelm Koehler, *Die Hofschule Karls des Grossen, Die karolingischen Miniaturen* 2 (Berlin, 1958), and more conveniently Florentine Mütherich and Joachim Gaehde, *Carolingian Painting* (New York, 1976), 7-9 and pls. 1-3.

33. The translation is again from Ganz, "Preconditions" (above, n.30). For the Latin text see Dümmler, ed., *PLAC* 1.91-92. The page is reproduced in the splendid facsimile publication, Kurt Holter, ed., *Der goldene Psalter "Dagulf-Psalter". Vollständige Faksimile-Ausgabe im Originalformat von Codex 1861 der Österreichischen Nationalbibliothek* (Graz, 1980), fol. 4r. For the manuscript, its date, and relationship to other of the so-called Court School group see my review of the facsimile publication in *Art Bulletin* 67 (1985): 681-690.

34. Peter Godman, *Poetry of the Carolingian Renaissance* (Norman, Oklahoma, 1985), esp. 9-16, and Dieter Schaller, "Poetic Rivalries at the Court of Charlemagne," in R.R. Bolgar, ed., *Classical Influences on European Culture 500-1500* (Cambridge, 1973), 151-157. I have discussed this issue at length in my *A Tainted Mantle: Hercules and the Classical Tradition at the Carolingian Court* (Philadelphia, 1991), with further references.

35. According to Bernard Bischoff, *Latin Palaeography. Antiquity and the Middle Ages,* trans. Dáibhí Ó Cróinín and David Ganz (Cambridge, 1990), 113: "it is inconceivable that fine scripts and able calligraphers would not have found recognition and encouragement [at Charlemagne's court]." Moreover, "from the verse dedications in the de luxe manuscripts written under Charlemagne's eyes by Godescalc and Dagulf... there speaks, besides loyalty, the pride of the artist."

36. The fundamental collection of the material remains the old study by J. Prochno, *Das Schreiber und Dedikationsbild in der deutschen Buchmalerei* (Leipzig and Berlin, 1929).

37. See Franz Ronig, *Codex Egberti: Der Perikopenbuch des Erzbischofs Egbert von Trier (977-993)* (Trier, 1977), 18 and fol. 2 for the donor portrait. For a discussion of the manuscript and of the important but anonymous "Gregory Master" who also contributed to it, see C.R. Dodwell, *Painting in Europe 800 to 1200* (Harmondsworth, 1971), 57-60, with further literature.

38. The image is in the Codex Vigilanus, named for the scribe Vigila, from the monastery of San Martín de Albelda (now Escorial, Bibliotebca del Monasterio, cod. d.I.2), and is dated 976; see for a discussion and for the important context of the work Jerrilynn Dodds, *Art and Ideology in Early Medieval Spain* (University Park, 1990), 80, with the earlier literature, and pl. 63.

39. Andrew Martindale, *The Rise of the Artist in the Middle Ages and Early Renaissance* (London, 1972), 68. Despite the sweep of the title, this book was originally conceived as a section of a book devoted to the "flowering of the Middle Ages," and therefore does not treat early medieval art and artists. For the Eadwine Psalter see C.R. Dodwell, *The Canterbury School of Illumination* (Cambridge, 1954), 36 and pl. 23, and for comments on the "creative copying" of an older work, see Hanns Swarzenski, "The Role of Copies in the Formation of the Styles of the Eleventh Century," *Romanesque and Gothic Art*, Studies in Western Art, Acts of the Twentieth International Congress of the History of Art 1 (Princeton, 1963), 9.

40. The compendious collection of scribal colophons is by the Benedictines of Le Bouveret, *Colophons des manuscrits occidentaux des origines au XVIe siècle*, 6 vols. (Fribourg, 1965-1982). An interesting collection and study is by Charles Plummer, "On the colophons and marginalia of Irish scribes," *Proceedings of the British Academy* 12 (1926): 11-44. For the modesty topos see the classic study by Ernst Robert Curtius, *European Literature and the Latin Middle Ages,* trans. Willard R. Trask (New York, 1953), 83-85.

41. Martindale, *Rise of the Artist* (above, n.39).

42. See for example Augustine, *The City of God* 19.25, discussed and with references in my *Tainted Mantle.*

43. For one of the fullest contemporary presentations of this concept, see the early twelfth-century treatise by "Theophilus" (Roger of Helmarshausen?), *The Various Arts, De diversis Artibus,* ed. and trans. C.R. Dodwell (Oxford, 1961), 1-4, with commentary that calls attention to the "unconscious irony" of Theophilus' opening sentence, in which he describes himself with the ancient papal title of "servus servorum Dei."

44. See Jean Leclercq, *The Love of Learning and the Desire for God. A Study of Monastic Culture,* trans. Catharine Misrahi (New York, 1961), passim.

45. See Robert Deshman, "The Exalted Servant: The Ruler Theology of the Prayerbook of Charles the Bald," *Viator* 11 (1980): 385-417, and idem, *"Benedictus Monarcha et Monachus.* Early Medieval Ruler Theology and the Anglo-Saxon Reform," *Frühmittelalterliche Studien* 22 (1988): 204-240.

46. Heinrich Klotz, "Formen der Anonymität und des Individualismus in der Kunst des Mittelalters und der Renaissance," *Gesta* 15 (1976): 303-31, referred to by Kessler, "State" (above, n.2), 180.

47. For some examples and further discussion of crosses associated with colophons see Lawrence Nees, "The Colophon Drawing in the Book of Mulling: A Supposed Irish Monastery Plan and the Tradition of Terminal Illustration in Early Medieval Manuscripts," *Cambridge Medieval Celtic Studies* 5 (1983):

67-91, especially 90. For a rare image of a self-portrait of the artist at the foot of the cross, which in this case, like the Valerianus Gospels image, is crowned by a bust of Christ, see Princeton Theological Seminary Library, cod. acc. no. 11.21.1900, fol. 1*r, in Gary Vikan, ed., *Illuminated Greek Manuscripts from American Collections* (Princeton, 1973), no. 26, 114-115. For donors at the foot of the cross see Deshman, "Exalted Servant."

48. For a convenient color reproduction of the entire cross page, with the very interesting colophon, and also for one of the pages with Greek lettering, see Jean Hubert, Jean Porcher and W. F. Volbach, *Europe of the Invasions,* trans. Stuart Gilbert and James Emmons (New York, 1969), figs.150 (the colophon) and 151.

49. For remarks on the magical connotations of books see my earlier studies, "Colophon Drawing," 85-88; "Two Illuminated Syriac Manuscripts in the Harvard College Library," *Cahiers archéologiques* 29 (1980-1981): 123-142, especially 132-142, and *The Gundohinus Gospels* (Cambridge, MA, 1987), 189-212.

50. For a brief description of the manuscript, with further bibliography, see *Karl der Grosse. Werk und Wirkung* (exhibition catalogue, Aachen, 1965), no. 439. One remarkable image on an eighth or early ninth-century single leaf in the St. Gall Stiftsbibliothek, cod. 1395, p. 418, shows a seated writer with pen and knife who has the unmistakable attribute of Christ, the crossed nimbus; see Jonathon J. G. Alexander, *Insular Manuscripts 6th to the 9th Century* (London, 1978), 79, no. 57, with further literature, and pl. 281. This feature of the miniature has commonly been dismissed as a mistake, but I think it possible to see it as a meaningful deliberate decision intending to show Christ himself as a scribe. The lengthy argument for such an interpretation must be offered in another place, however. I addressed this issue in a lecture entitled "The Irish Manuscripts at St. Gall and their Continental Affiliations," at a conference on "The Arts and Letters in Medieval and Baroque St. Gall Viewed from the Late Twentieth Century"; the proceedings of the conference are to be published and edited by the conference organizer, James C. King.

51. For the inspired Evangelist type see Carl Nordenfalk, "Der inspirierte Evangelist," *Wiener Jahrbuch für Kunstgeschichte* 36 (1983): 175-190, with many illustrations and extensive bibliography. For a classic statement of the Neoplatonic sources of Renaissance ideas see Erwin Panofsky, "The Neoplatonic Movement and Michelangelo," in his *Studies in Iconology. Humanistic Themes in the Art of the Renaissance* (Oxford, 1939), 171-230; see however for criticism of this approach Bredekamp, "Götterdämmerung des Neuplatonismus" (above, n.20). A fascinating study of the topic of evangelical inspiration from the Middle Ages into the early seventeenth century is Irving

Lavin, "Divine Inspiration in Caravaggio's Two *St. Matthews*," *Art Bulletin* 56 (1974): 59-81.

52. Drawing by Jack Ziegler, *The New Yorker* (August 11, 1975), 69.

53. See Dümmler, ed., *PLAC* 2.186, here quoted and with the translation by Peter Godman, *Poetry*, 248-249.

54. The illustration here is taken from the manuscript in Vienna, Österreich-ische Nationalbibliothek, cod. 652, fol. 33v, dating from later in the ninth century. For the manuscript see Kurt Holter, ed., *Hrabanus Maurus. Liber de laudibus sanctae crucis. Codex Vindobonensis 652 der Österreichischen Nationalbibliothek, Wien. Vollständige Faksimile-Ausgabe* (Graz, 1972). On *carmina figurata* of this work in general, and on this portrait image in particular, see now Elizabeth Sears, "Word and Image in Carolingian *Carmina Figurata*," in Irving Lavin, ed., *World Art. Themes of Unity in Diversity*, Acts of the 26th International Congress of the History of Art 2 (University Park and London, 1989), 340-345, and the important theological analysis by Celia Martin Chazelle, *The Cross, the Image, and the Passion in Carolingian Thought and Art* (Ph.D. dissertation, Yale University, 1985), 181-185.

55. See for a recent general study based very largely upon written sources Dodwell, *Anglo-Saxon Art* (above, n.26).

56. See Julian Brown's discussion of this point in Thomas D. Kendrick, T. Julian Brown, R.L.S. Bruce-Mitford, et al., *Evangeliorum quattuor Codex Linsdisfarnensis* (Olten/Lausanne, 1960), 5-11.

57. See Anderson, "Theodore Psalter," 558.

58. On the notion of the avant-garde see the remarks by Belting, *End of the History of Art?* (above, n.8), 12-15, with earlier literature; to this may now be added Rosalind Kraus, *The Originality of the Avant-Garde and Other Modernist Myths* (Cambridge, MA, 1985).

59. See David H. Wright, "Some Notes on English Uncial," *Traditio* 17 (1961): 441-456.

60. Obviously I here oversimplify the Morellian method expounded in such works as his *Italian Masters in German Galleries*, trans. (from German) by Louise M. Richter (London, 1883); see here especially p.191 for drawings of ears by Palma Vecchio and the two Bonifazios, and p.219 for ears by Leonardo and Lorenzo di Credi. See also Bernard Berenson, "The Rudiments of Connoisseurship," in *The Study and Criticism of Italian Art*, Second Series (London, 1901), 111-148. Morelli and Berenson and their followers certainly grant the importance of many other factors beside such taxonomy in the determination of authorship. See now for a recent assessment Sydney J. Freedberg, "Berenson, Connoisseurship, and the History of Art," *The New Criterion* 7, no. 6 (February, 1989): 7-16.

61. For a brief review of the formulations of the concept of style in art historical literature see Belting, *End of the History of Art?* (above, n.8), 26-29, with extensive literature, with the comment (28) that "the old notion of a style traveling on a one-way street of formal development has collapsed."

62. I by no means intend to deny the evident fact of stylistic development, which remains a useful and indeed essential concept. Distinguished recent studies that attempt to trace stylistic development are, however, un-Rieglian in allowing for the impact of changes in political and social conditions, functions, and many other factors; see for example Ernst Kitzinger, *Byzantine Art in the Making. Main Lines of Stylistic Development in Mediterranean Art, 3rd-7th century* (Cambridge, MA, 1977).

63. Helmut Roth, *Kunst der Völkerwanderungszeit,* Propyläen Kunstgeschichte, suppl. 4 (Frankfurt, 1979), 155 and 162, pl. 75.

64. See Edward James, *The Franks* (Oxford, 1988).

65. Bernhard Salin, *Die altgermanische Thierornamentik: Typologische Studien über germanische Metallgegenstände aus dem IV. bis IX. Jahrhunderts, nebst einer Studie über irische Ornamentik,* trans. (from Swedish) by J. Mestorf (Stockholm, 1904).

66. See Haseloff, "Germanische Tierstil" (above, n.28).

67. R.L.S. Bruce-Mitford, *The Art of the Codex Amiatinus,* Jarrow Lecture 1967 (Jarrow-upon-Tyne, 1967), also published in *Journal of the British Archaeological Assocation,* 3rd ser., 32 (1969): 1-25.

68. Per Jonas Nordhagen, *The Codex Amiatinus and the Byzantine Element in the Northumbrian Renaissance,* Jarrow Lecture, 1977 (Jarrow-on-Tyne, 1977).

69. For a convenient recent discussion of the manuscript as a whole and of this miniature, see Janet Backhouse, *The Lindisfarne Gospels* (Ithaca, 1981), with further literature, especially the fundamental but to many inaccessible study by R.L.S. Bruce-Mitford, "Decoration and Miniatures," in Kendrick, et al., *Codex Lindisfarnensis,* 107-260, esp. 142-173.

70. See Swarzenski, "Role of Copies" (above, n.39), 7-18.

71. For a convenient English translation of this text see Cyril Mango, *The Art of the Byzantine Empire 312-1453,* Sources and Documents in the History of Art (Englewood Cliffs, NJ, 1972), 72-78.

72. Richard Krautheimer, *Early Christian and Byzantine Architecture* (Harmondsworth, 1965), 158.

73. W. Eugene Kleinbauer, "Pre-Carolingian Concepts of Architectural Planning," in Marilyn J. Chiat and Kathryn L. Reyerson, eds., *The Medieval Mediterranean. Cross-Cultural Contacts*, Medieval Studies at Minnesota 3 (St. Cloud, Minnesota, 1988), 67-79, especially 74.

74. Kleinbauer, "Pre-Carolingian Concepts," loc. cit.

75. Mildred Budny and Dominic Tweddle, "The Early Medieval Textiles at Maaseik, Belgium," *The Antiquaries Journal* 65 (1985): 353-389.

76. R.L.S. Bruce-Mitford, et al., *The Sutton Hoo Ship-Burial* 2, *Arms, Armour and Regalia* (London, 1978).

77. Bruce-Mitford, *Sutton Hoo* 2. 523-535, pls. 15-18, and figs.386-393 on the shoulder clasps. There is a very interesting problem posed by the fact that no one but the wearer could have properly seen these newly "recognizable" animals, but that observation leads far from the present context, and deserves fuller exploration in another place.

78. See the complete facsimile reproduction of the manuscript, Koert van der Horst and Jacobus H.A. Engelbregt, eds., *Utrecht-Psalter. Vollständige Faksimile-Ausgabe im Originalformat der Handschrift 32 aus dem Besitz der Bibliotheek der Rijksuniversiteit te Utrecht* (Graz, 1984), with earlier literature, especially on this question Suzy Dufrenne, *Les illustrations du psautier d'Utrecht: Sources et apport carolingien* (Paris, 1978).

79. See Joachim Gaehde, "The Draughtsmen of the Utrecht Psalter," in Katharina Bierbrauer, Peter K. Klein and Willibald Sauerländer, eds., *Studien zur mittelalterlichen Kunst 800-1250* (Munich, 1985), 49-52, with earlier bibliography.

80. For beautiful color plates of both the Doubting Thomas and paired Moses ivories, see Danielle Gaborit-Chopin, *Elfenbeinkunst im Mittelalter*, trans. (from French) by Gisela Bloch and Roswitha Beyer (Berlin, 1978), cat. no. 95, with earlier bibliography, and pl. 97.

81. For the miniature of the tenth century in Leningrad see Vera Dmitrieva Likhachova, *Vizantiiskaia miniatura (Byzantine Miniatures)* (Moscow, 1977), pl. 6, and Victor Lazarev, *Storia della pittura bizantina*, trans. Gildo Fossati (Turin, 1967), 139-140 and pl. 116. For the Byzantine ivory, at Dumbarton Oaks, see Kurt Weitzmann, *Ivories and Steatites*, Catalogue of the Byzantine and Early Medieval Antiquities in the Dumbarton Oaks Collection 3 (Washington, 1972), no. 21.

82. Gaborit-Chopin, *Elfenbeinkunst*, pl. 76.

83. The date, point of origin, and context of this new Crucifixion iconography remain difficult questions. It had long been thought that the earliest instances and origin could be placed in the ninth century, with some scholars favoring an eastern and some a western context. For this approach, see Chazelle, *The Cross, the Image, and the Passion,* especially 342-354 and n.334 with earlier literature. More recently several authors have put forward pictorial and textual evidence for an earlier origin, in the late seventh or eighth century, specifically in connection with eastern doctrinal disputes. For a presentation of this approach see Anna Kartsonis, *Anastasis. The Making of an Image* (Princeton, 1986), 40-52, with references to the earlier literature.

84. Robert Deshman, "*Christus rex et magi reges:* Kingship and Christology in Ottonian and Anglo-Saxon Art," *Frühmittelalterliche Studien* 10 (1976): 367-405, especially 368-377.

85. See also Deshman, "*Benedictus Monarcha et Monachus*" (above, n.45), with the Aachen image of Otto III illustrated as fig.49, the earlier bibliography concerning it given as n.2, to which may now be added Gerhart B. Ladner, *L'immagine dell' imperatore Ottone III* (Rome, 1988). It is worth noting here that although the specific iconographic form, the artistic invention in the narrower sense, is quite distinct for the Otto III miniature, the depiction of the same ruler "in majesty" was adopted for his official seals in 997, a distinct but similarly startling departure from all previous iconographic formulations. For the seal see Erich Kittel, *Siegel* (Brunswick, 1970), 210 and fig.128.

86. See Nancy Netzer, *The Trier Gospels* (Ph.D. dissertation, Harvard University, 1986). The miniature was more briefly discussed by George Henderson, *From Durrow to Kells. The Insular Gospel-books 650-800* (London, 1987), fig.104 and p.75: "The image again suggests an experiment in visualizing the Evangelists in terms of tetramorphs, with bizarre results."

87. Henderson, *From Durrow to Kells,* 43 and fig.42, with earlier bibliography.

88. Henderson, *From Durrow to Kells,* fig.130.

89. Carlo Cecchelli, Giuseppe Furlani, and Mario Salmi, *The Rabbula Gospels: Facsimile Edition of the Miniatures of the Syriac Manuscript Plut. I. 56 in the Medicean-Laurentian Library,* Monumenta Occidentis 1 (Olten and Lausanne, 1959).

90. The same scribe wrote the same formula, "Thomas scribsit," beneath his portrait of the evangelist Luke (fol. 125v), illustrated by Alexander, *Insular Manuscripts* (above, n.50), no. 26, fig.113. That he chose to associate his signature with an evangelist portrait that he had painted supports the

identification previously suggested. I have no explanation for the choice of Luke only for this association, but the association of Luke with painting goes back at least as far as the sixth century, although it is generally thought to have become a commonplace in the west from the twelfth; see remarks by Jean Owens Schaefer, "Saint Luke as Painter: From Saint to Artisan to Artist," in Barral i Altet, ed., *Artistes, artisans et production artistique* (above, n.29), 1:413-429. It should be pointed out that the scribe Thomas of the Trier Gospels also wrote his name next to that of his apostolic namesake in the canon table series of the manuscript; none of the other apostles are so inscribed, and Thomas alone is beardless and with a monastic tonsure, so again it seems clear that some identification with the scribe is intended.

91. See Walter Horn and Ernest Born, *The Plan of St. Gall. A Study of the Architecture and Economy of, and Life in a Paradigmatic Carolingian Monastery*, 3 vols. (Berkeley, 1979). For a different perspective from that of the authors on the question of the plan as original or copy, see my "The Plan of St. Gall and the Theory of the Program of Carolingian Art," *Gesta* 25 (1986): 1-8, with extensive earlier bibliography.

92. Horn and Born, *Plan of St. Gall*, 1:xx, and Adalbert de Vogüé, "Le Plan de Saint-Gall, copie d'un document officiel? Une lecture de la lettre à Gozbert," *Revue bénédictine* 94 (1984): 295-314.

93. See the convenient brief discussion by Howard Hibbard, *Bernini* (Baltimore, 1965), 128-141, which mentions some pictorial precedents for the composition.

94. Oxford, Bodleian Library, cod. Auct. F. 4.32, fol. 1r. For a facsimile publication see R.W. Hunt, *Saint Dunstan's Classbook from Glastonbury. Codex Biblioth. Bodleianae Oxon. Auct. F. 4/32*, Umbrae codicum occidentalium 4 (Amsterdam, 1961). According to Hunt, "the form of the words... suggests that St. Dunstan was responsible for them. Whether he was also responsible for the drawing it is impossible to say, but there is nothing inherently improbable in the hypothesis." A convenient recent discussion with earlier literature is Elzbieta Temple, *Anglo-Saxon Manuscripts 900-1066*, A Survey of Manuscripts Illuminated in the British Isles 2 (London, 1976), no. 11.

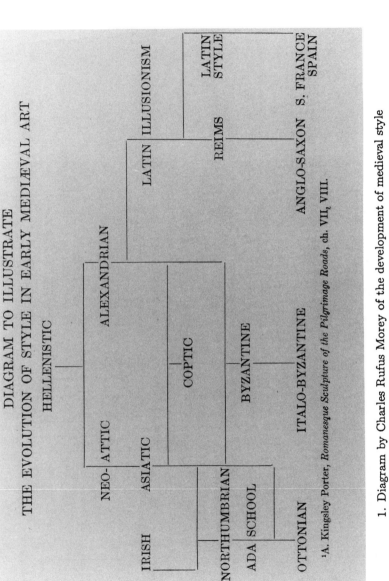

1. Diagram by Charles Rufus Morey of the development of medieval style

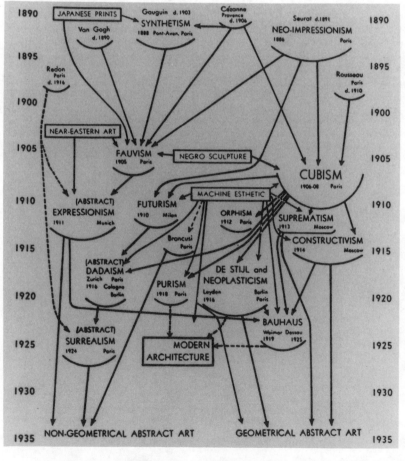

2. Diagram by Alfred Barr of the development of modern art

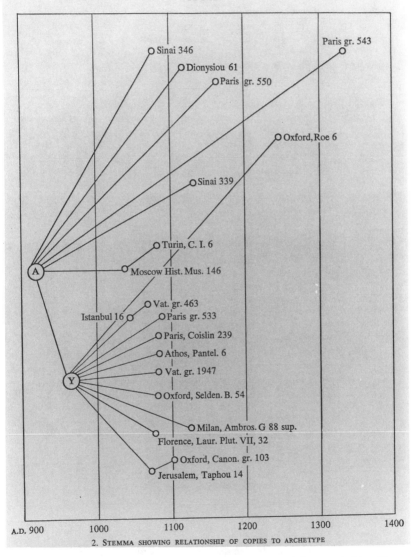

Sinai 346

Dionysiou 61

Paris gr. 550

Paris gr. 543

Oxford, Roe 6

Sinai 339

Turin, C. I. 6

Moscow Hist. Mus. 146

A

Vat. gr. 463

Istanbul 16

Paris gr. 533

Paris, Coislin 239

Athos, Pantel. 6

Vat. gr. 1947

Y

Oxford, Selden. B. 54

Milan, Ambros. G 88 sup.

Florence, Laur. Plut. VII, 32

Oxford, Canon. gr. 103

Jerusalem, Taphou 14

A.D. 900   1000   1100   1200   1300   1400

2. STEMMA SHOWING RELATIONSHIP OF COPIES TO ARCHETYPE

3. Diagram by George Galavaris of the manuscripts of Gregory's Homilies

196. Pag. 305: Gregory of Nyssa   197. Pag. 365: Joseph   198. Pag. 382: Zechariah

199. Pag. 6: John the Faster   201. Pag. 216: Nahum

200. Pag. 299: Peter and Andrew

196-201. VATICAN. Cod. gr. 1613

4. Comparison of illuminators in the Menologion of Basil II
(after Weitzmann)

5. Wittislingen brooch, front.
Prähistorische Sammlung, Munich

6. Wittislingen brooch, rear with inscription by Wigerig.
Prähistorische Sammlung, Munich

7. Godescalc Gospel Lectionary, colophon page.
Paris, BN, n.a. lat. 1203, f. 126v

8. Godescalc Gospel Lectionary, Evangelist John and Christ.
Paris, BN, n.a. lat. 1203, f. 2v-3r

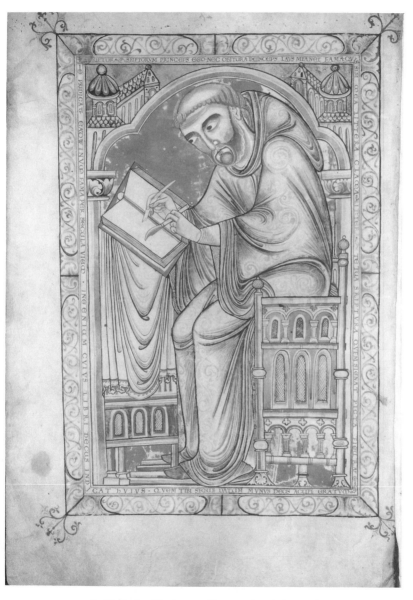

9. Eadwine Psalter, self-portrait of the scribe.
Cambridge, Trinity College, cod. 17.1, f. 283v

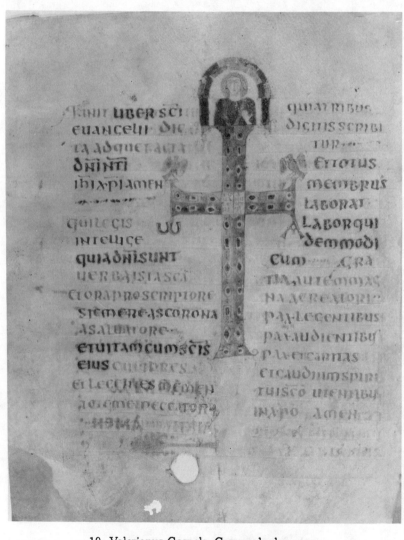

10. Valerianus Gospels, Cross-colophon page.
Munich, Clm. 6224, f. 202v

11. Flavigny Gospels, Christ and Evangelists page.
Autun, BM, MS 4, f. 8r

"Hey, I'm thirsty. I need a drink. A drink and a liverwurst sandwich. Hey, how about a sandwich and a beer down at Gallagher's, and then we can go shoot some pool? Or maybe take in a movie. Hey, I'm talking to you."

12. Jack Ziegler, drawing of writer with angelic inspiration

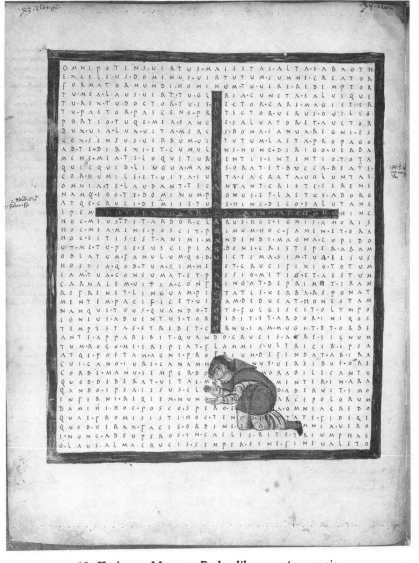

13. Hrabanus Maurus, *De laudibus sanctae crucis*,
Monk kneeling before cross. Vienna, ÖNB, cod. 652, f. 33v

14. Ostrogothic eagle fibula from Domagnano.
National Museum, Nuremberg

CODICIBVS SACRIS HOSTILI CLADE PERVSTIS
ESDRA DŌ FERVENS HOC REPARAVIT OPVS

15. Codex Amiatinus, Prophet Ezra.
Florence, Bibl. Med.-Laur., cod. Amiatino 1, f. Vr

16. Lindisfarne Gospels, Evangelist Matthew.
London, BL, cod. Cotton Nero D. IV, f. 25v

17. Sutton Hoo ship burial, hinged clasp.
British Museum, London

18. Incredulity of Thomas, ivory from Echternach.
Staatliche Museen Preussischer Kulturbesitz, Berlin

19. Incredulity of Thomas, ivory from Constantinople.
Dumbarton Oaks, Washington, D.C.

20. Crucifix, ivory from Trier.
Schatkamer, Sint Servaaskerk, Maastricht

21. Liuthard Gospels of Otto III, Emperor in Majesty.
Aachen, Domschatz, f. 16r

22. Trier Gospels, Tetramorph.
Trier, Domschatz, cod. 61, f. 5v

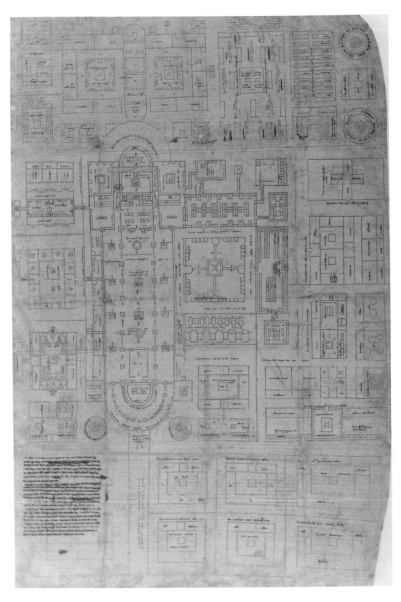

23. Plan of St. Gall.
St. Gall, Stiftsbibl., cod. 1092

24. Gian Lorenzo Bernini, Ecstasy of S. Teresa.
Cornaro Chapel, S. Maria della Vittoria, Rome

25. St. Dunstan's Classbook, St. Dunstan kneeling before Christ.
Oxford, Bodleian, cod. Auct. F.4.32, f. 1r

About the Editor:

Celia Chazelle is an independent scholar residing in Princeton, NJ. She received her B.A. from the University of Toronto in 1977 and her Ph.D. from Yale University in 1985. She specializes in early medieval culture, has written articles on Carolingian theology and iconography, and is working on a monograph on Carolingian literature and imagery relating to the cross and the crucifixion. Current projects also include a critical edition of texts by Alcuin of York, on which she is collaborating with Professors John Cavadini of the University of Notre Dame and E. Ann Matter of the University of Pennsylvania.

About the Contributors:

Seth Lerer has been Professor of English at Stanford University since 1990. He received his Ph.D. from the University of Chicago in 1981, and taught at Princeton University from 1981-1990. He is the author of *Boethius and Dialogue: Literary Method in the Consolation of Philosophy* (Princeton, 1985) and *Literacy and Power in Anglo-Saxon Literature* (Lincoln, NE, 1991). He has recently completed a further study, *Chaucer and his Readers: Imagining the Author in Late Medieval England.*

Thomas Noble is Associate Professor of History at the University of Virginia, a faculty which he joined in 1980. He received his Ph.D. from Michigan State under Professor Richard E. Sullivan in 1974 and is the author of *The Republic of St. Peter: The Birth of the Papal State, 680-825* (Philadelphia, 1984) as well as the editor, with John J. Contreni, of *Religion, Culture, and Society in the Early Middle Ages: Studies in Honor of Richard E. Sullivan* (Kalamazoo, Michigan, 1987). His current field of research is theology and politics in the reign of Charlemagne, with a particular regard to images in the Carolingian world.

Lawrence Nees is Professor of Art History at the University of Delaware. He received his B.A. from the University of Chicago in 1970, and his Ph.D. from Harvard University in 1977. His specialty is early medieval art history. He has written *The Gundohinus Gospels* (Cambridge, MA, 1987), *A Tainted Mantle: Hercules and the Classical Tradition at the Carolingian Court* (Philadelphia, 1991), and the annotated bibliography *From Justinian to Charlemagne. European Art, A.D. 565-787* (Boston, 1985).